- Enjoy Yourself -
It's
Later Than You
Think

By
Michael Levy

MIND, BODY, SOUL
Time is of the essence
No time to worry
Begin a new life
Adopt a different view
This book will reveal the real you

WHAT IS THE POINT 3

© Copyright 1999 by Point of Life, Inc.

All rights reserved.

No part of this publication may be reproduced or transmitted in any form, or by any means, electronic, mechanical, including photocopy, recording, or any information storage and retrieval system, without permission in writing from the publisher.

Requests for permission to make copies of any part of the work should be mailed to Permissions Dept., Point of Life, Inc., P.O. Box 7017, West Palm Beach, FL 33405, or contact us on the web at www.pointoflife.com.

The opinions expressed in this book are those of the author. He is not medically qualified, and any opinions given are based on his life experiences. Readers should consult a medical professional before making any changes to medications, exercise regimens, diet or other health related issues.

First Printing, May 1999

ISBN 0-9668069-2-1

Printed in the United States of America

Table of Contents

About the Author	6
Acknowledgement	7
Preface	8
Introduction	9
What Gives Joy	11
Spider's Web – Cobweb	12
A Waste of Time	15
The Movies	16
A Summer Trust	18
The Chosen Planet	19
Beginning of Solutions	21
Mankind Discovers	24
The Universe	25
God's Place	26
The Dark	27
The Speed of Dark	29
Blowing Bubbles	31
Treasures of the Universe	34
A Pure Diamond	35
Crystal Minds	37
Glory Visions	39
Almighty on Line	41
The Subconscious Soul	42
The One and Only	44
When are we Going to Learn	46
No Time	48
Unconditioned Love	50
All Souls	53
Senses of the Soul	54
The Land Where Souls Play	57
Ego's With Taboos	58
The Morals of Man	59
A Change of View	63

Life Is Beautiful	65
True Values	66
My Spirit's Voice	67
Smile Please, This is the Real Candid Camera	70
The Fruitful Life	72
Shopping Basket	73
Tough Luck	74
Distortion of Faith	77
Remain a Bright Light	80
Be A Spring	83
A Long-Term Investor	84
Negative Junkie	86
Martyrs To Worry	87
Poor Little Rich Girl	89
Boomerang	91
No Hopers	93
Dreams of Hope	94
Everything	96
The Show of the Season	98
A Positive and Negative Balance	99
The Gravy Train	100
God's Real Cool	102
The Town Crier	103
Looking for the Light	105
Man and Tree	106
On Reflection	108
Party Time	110
No Quick Fixes	111
Life in a Bottle	113
It's a Jungle Out There	116
Blue Chip Brain Waves	118
The Wind	120
Faced with Joy!	122
Play the Game – Round One	124
Risky Lies	126
Playing a Round	128

Play the Game – Round Two	129
The Magic Elixir	132
Time is a Bargain	133
Crops of Thought	135
Conclusion	136
Book of Proverbs	137
The Joy of Life	141

About the Author

Michael Levy was born in Manchester, England, in 1945. This is his third book to be published in nine months. He started writing in August 1998. Michael's other books are:

Minds of Blue, Souls of Gold
What is the Point

Michael's view of life is that nobody needs to worry. Worrying is a self-inflicted punishment that has been conditioned as an inevitable way to live. This should not be the case. Through Michael's books, you will be able to have a choice of staying the same as you are now or living life as it was meant to be lived -- in Joy and Harmony.

Every day is a learning experience for Michael; and each day he realizes how little he knows. If we make it half way up the ladder of wisdom in our lifetime, we would be very wise indeed.

Read this book over and over until you live it.

Acknowledgement

I realize that I am merely a vessel that is used by the Cosmic Flow of all things. My memories are intertwined with messages of wisdom from a source of energy that has created and evolved all things.

I would like to thank the Creator for allowing me to be the vehicle to express these words of wisdom. These words will allow each of us to go through life with joy and bliss, and to enjoy the life we deserve.

I dedicate this book to my wife Margaret. She has been an inspiration and motivator in helping me produce three books in less than nine months.

Thank you for purchasing this book and may all your days be happy ones.

Preface

Many taboo subjects exist in our society. There are many things we do not talk about, as we find them distasteful. In this book I have put into context certain aspects of our lives that conform to societies rules but are not as nature intended.

Many people are kept alive by medications and operations. There is a better way of handling our physical presence on this Earth without help from the Medical Establishment. They do a wonderful job after we have allowed our bodies to deteriorate, but it is so much better to alleviate the stress and strains of modern living by the correct thought process.

When I refer to mankind in this book, it also includes all women. For the ease of writing I use "man" or "mankind" to encompass all humans. We are a Spiritual being experiencing a human life form. God has instructed us to enjoy the experience. Who wants to argue with GOD?

Introduction

True joy does not radiate from the materialistic world. We exist to enjoy our time on earth to the fullest. This does not mean running around like a "chicken with it's head cut off" looking for man-made pleasures. Nothing in the physical sense lasts. Finding the correct formula to exist in joy at this moment is everyone's desire.

Having a limited amount of time in our physical form poses the question "Do we want to live with a fit mind and body or one that is out of condition?" We have a choice.

If we choose to have a fit mind and body, then we will probably get a longer, more enjoyable life span. No guarantees, but we increase the odds in our favor. Eating sensible foods -- fruits, vegetables, grains, nuts, etc. -- ensures good nutrition. Regular exercise ensures strong lungs, heart and muscle tone. Physical fitness amounts to twenty percent of our well being. Now for the remaining 80% - we need to have a fit mind.

Taking care of our thought process takes careful consideration. Leaving it to chance by allowing other wrongly conditioned humans to educate us is not to be recommended. Many people are in a constant sleep during their lives. They become transfixed in a zombie state of mind -- excepting all types of do's and don'ts as the normal way to live. To adopt this way of thinking will lead to many mishaps and perhaps an early grave.

When someone is starving we can send him or her food. If we continually send food, they become reliant on us. If we send them seeds and tools to plant -- with a set of instructions on how to irrigate and harvest -- then they can become self-sufficient. In today's world, we need wisdom. Intellect is not enough to overcome the pitfalls of the modern world.

My book is written in an easy to understand manner. Although you may not agree with all that is written, one fact remains -- if you start to change the way you think, you will increase your life span and enjoy the remainder of your physical form here on this wonderful earth.

WHAT GIVES JOY

Only joy was meant to be,
a dog gives joy to a flea,
the honeysuckle rose, gives joy to a bee,
water from clouds, gives joy to the tree.

The taste of bananas, gives joy to the monkey,
thoughts of a carrot, gives joy to a donkey,
being a Judge, gives the joy of a plea,
opening the door gives joy, when we find the key.

Wages of toil gives joy to the worker,
being on the dole gives joy to the shirker,
living in a mist gives joy when life becomes clearer,
living in old age gives joy, life becomes dearer and dearer.

Just being alive gives joy, we are natures miracle,
being on earth gives joy, we are a curve in the circle,
inspiration of Spirit gives joy, our dreams fulfill,
Gods divine love gives joy, in eternity time stands still.

M. L.

Spider's Web - Cobweb

"Come into my parlor" said the spider to the fly. The fly happily whizzes around the house unaware the spider is busy weaving his sticky strands into a web that will trap and eat him. The spider is a genius at weaving a web - so is the Devil's evil. The fly's fast movements and unawareness of the danger of an almost invisible silky web land him right on a sticky strand. Once his body touches the strand, his fate is sealed. The more he struggles to free himself, the more entangled he becomes. The spider watches the fly tire himself out then comes along and devours him with no effort.

The only work the spider has to do is weave its web of destruction. He leaves his trap open to catch the fly and then spins another web elsewhere. Before we know it, spider traps have been spun all over the place. We all know that flies have very quick reflexes. When we try and swat a fly, most times the fly senses danger and flies away. The webs are stationary and almost invisible. The fly is not aware of this danger.

When we arrive on the Earth we have complete freedom of thought, we have joy and happiness, and can whiz around without any restrictions to our joy. We learn about the physical dangers around us and we avoid them. Our reflexes are very good at dodging dangers in most instances. A few accidents happen. For example, a small percentage of people are killed in road accidents because their awareness had faulted; but overall, car accidents cause only a very small percent of deaths. Far more people die from illness than anything else, and most illnesses are caused by the mind.

A worry is a strand in the web. Once our minds become ensnared on a sticky worry, that is the beginning of our downfall. We have been snarled in a worry trap. Worries often lead to phobias and restrictions on leading a joyful life. This leads to anxiety and fear, then we entrap ourselves in jealousy and hatred.

Even if the spider (death) does not devour us, all these negatives consume our life. The web we have become wrapped up in was not meant to be. *We have woven our own traps.*

Nature is a wonder. What happens when a spider's web is left? It becomes a cobweb. Dust all around the web has taken all the stickiness away by surrounding each strand. The cobweb is harmless, but it is unsightly. Nobody wants to see a lot of cobwebs, so we spring clean. We get out our feather duster and clear them all away. Dust is a fly's best friend -- it reveals the trap the spider set and now it is no longer a threat.

The dust we can sprinkle in our mind is *"Soul Dust."* It was Stardust originally; after many billions of years, it has turned up in our bodies. All of our body is formed from Stardust. The most important part is our *"Soul Dust."* Once we allow it to coat our minds, no worry or fear will be trapped in our thoughts. All the old thoughts can now be seen for what they are -- traps to take away our happiness and put us in an early grave.

That is unsightly and messy so we will spring clean them away using *"Spirit"* as our duster. We then find that our *"Soul Dust"* is *"Go(l)d Dust"* - *"God dust."* What a wonderful dust to have our brains coated with.

A worry cannot be seen. It is invisible to the eye and an awareness is not enough to stop it from entrapping us. All our thoughts are invisible. No machine has been invented to read our minds. We have to be able to recondition a web of negative traps. *"God Dust"* now turns to *"God Trust"* and that is what we must do. *Trust ourselves to believe in ourselves. To love ourselves, this means loving God. We are God in our invisible thoughts. This is as close as any human can get to an understanding of a Soul.*

Soul is God inside our physical form. If man does not want to acknowledge this, then man is a fly in the web of a negative life waiting to be devoured by worry.

Time is of the essence. We do not want to waste a second living like a fly.

A WASTE OF TIME

Moments passing by, the ticking of a clock,
never coming back, gift that humans mock,
time and tide continue their relentless pace,
shadows lengthen on the brow of a worried face.

More precious than any jewel,
only to be squandered by the proverbial fool,
The wasted days, lost in ego's maze,
anxiety and fear, feed the waifs and strays.

Flotsam and jetsam, wash upon the shore,
empty vessels, with no sight of a cure,
the Devil's fisherman, using restlessness as a lure,
turning the hours, into a boring humdrum chore.

A second missed, no second chance,
only joy, will the minutes enhance,
sunrise, sunset, swings and roundabouts,
time for your journey, the grim reaper shouts.

M.L.

The Movies

We have all gone to the movies and watched a sentimental or sad story unfold. As the film progresses, we begin to cry. By the end of the movie, we are sobbing away. How can we cry at celluloid film? It is only light projected on a screen showing photo images moving and talking. When we immerse ourselves in the story we become attached to the characters. It could be an animal. It could even be a cartoon character. A movie producer's 'ace card' is sentimentality.

Think of the saddest movie you have ever seen. Now we are going to view it from a different angle. We start at the end of the movie and we see a pile of dust. No one is crying. The next scene is a funeral. Still no tears. The next scene is a hospital bed. Still no tears. The next scene is watching a person leading up to an illness. We feel concern but we do not know the character well enough to cry over it. As the scene progresses backwards, we do become more involved with the story. However, all the sad stuff has gone and we were detached from the story so we did not feel the sadness.

We are all going to end as a pile of dust. If we understand this in its true context, then we realize we return from where we came. This is in the physical and *"Spiritual"* form. If we reverse our attachments to the physical we just enjoy the *"Spiritual."* This is our true identity. When we act out this way of thinking, we can return to the physical and just enjoy it while we have it. Joy and love with no attachment means no worry, no anxiety, no fear, no negativity.

Let us go back to the movies and watch the funniest film we have ever viewed. When we play this backward it is funny right away. It does not matter if the story is played backwards.

Funny scenes just make us laugh and even if we are not attached to the characters, we still find this amusing. The same happens with a joyful film. If the end of the movie is a party scene, we immediately get into the festive *Spirit* and enjoy watching (even though we watch the scenes backwards). Reversing joy and happiness still leaves joy and happiness. Reversing sorrow and sentimentality leaves a more fundamental view of life without tears.

In the Chinese culture, they mourn the birth of a baby and rejoice a death. Their philosophy is simple - when we are born, we will endure all the hardships of the physical world. Only when we die will we have contentment and peace. This way of thinking may seem strange to the Western World but it has merit and logic. We grow towards death from the moment we are conceived. Our body strengthens until we get to a certain age, then it begins to deteriorate. Our physical life span is short; so if we look forward with joy to the day we die, this relieves us of the fear of death. As for the non- rejoicing at birth, it gets the negative side of life out of the way and the older we get the more we can rejoice.

The real secret is to enjoy birth and death equally. There are no downside elements to life unless we allow it to be so. The Chinese come closest to achieving this philosophy but it still has its basics in man-made doctrines and customs, and at best limits the divine blissfulness we all deserve to experience.

Controlling our emotions and sensitivity to focus on the blissfulness of physical existence becomes easier; especially the more we understand that our *Spiritual* life is eternal and can guide and control our emotions. We need to live in peace, contentment, love and joy. We then carry these sensations on forever. Whereas, all that is left in the physical material sense is a heap of dust.

A SUMMER TRUST

Showers in April,
wow, what a thrill,
moving stream from still,
reservoir to fill.

A spring day in May,
sun shining, making hay,
savoring the joy in every way,
participating in nature's play.

A summer's day in June,
Lovers on a honeymoon,
under the moon they swoon,
precious moments pass far too soon.

Birds soaring high in July,
currents of heat, gliding in the sky,
flowers and perfume my! oh my!,
exaltations of senses, see how they fly.

Hours of fun in August,
do we have to like it, yes we must,
we have no time, to be all fussed,
our Soul invested in God's irrevocable trust.
M.L.

The Chosen Planet

A few thousand years ago (a blink in Cosmic terms) a man received a message that the Hebrews were "the chosen people" to spread God's word. The message was distorted and over a period of time, many religions have sprung up and caused tremendous pain and suffering by dividing the world of mankind. Religion has detoured mankind's mission. The focus on prayer and paying homage to God has taken away our true purpose of life here on earth. By separating humans into different groups, it seemingly delayed the natural evolution of the Universe.

The Earth is in an ideal position in the Universe to sustain a multitude of life forms. The gravitational pull is perfect. The distance from the Sun is perfect. The distance from the Moon is perfect. The temperature is perfect. This all plays a part in allowing Earth to blossom and grow. The message the man received a few thousand years ago was: *The Planet Earth has been chosen as the Planet to sustain life throughout the whole of our Universe by ONE GOD. IT IS THE CHOSEN PLANET.*

The cosmos is infinite, and although our Universe is enormous and keeps expanding, it is only one of many. So Earth is the chosen Planet. What is our role in all of this? There has to be a Master Plan or a blueprint showing how humans can be a strong link in the chain of evolution and creation. *We exist to live in joy.*

All living entities are here to enjoy. That is not a mission, I here you say. *Correct -- our mission is to transfer physical matter to Planets who are not as fortunate as Earth and do not have the natural ability to sustain life.*

Other planets lack gravity, light, oxygen and have huge temperature variations. While we are looking for life on those planets, man should really be working out ways to bring physical life to these places.

BEGINNING OF SOLUTIONS

An ocean of stars, galaxies of "Blue Waves"
ebbing and flowing, within a Cosmic haze,
billions of light years, joined in dimensions of space,
ever evolving formations, timelessness sets the pace.

Fuzzy logic chips, guiding artificial intelligence,
processors that cannot reason, programmed by man's sense,
conscious minds, with problems to be sought,
prying questions, a penny for your thought.

Pools of information, flooding from outer space,
intense bio feedback, not one drop to waste,
Codes sent by Universal keyboards, perpetual information stored,
robots in cyberspace, computers self-assured.

Molecules of neurons, transported to a distant Planet,
signals of all the signs, spinning heads that plan it,
seas of many infusions, free the brain's pollutions,
vastness to explore, the beginning of solutions.

M.L.

There already is a *Spiritual* life in the whole of space. "Invisible Intelligence" is everywhere. Earth will be the basis for all physical life forms throughout the Universe. The Hi-Tech revolution going on now is the beginning of a new age of enlightenment in all that exists. We have learned how to clone physical life forms. Genetic technology is advancing at a fast pace. We are building faster working computers. All this intelligence is for a purpose.

Why have we had to suffer famine and drought? Why so many wars? Why so many life-taking storms, volcanic eruptions? Why so many murders, crimes of hate, persecutions? Why death by accident, illness, cruelty? Why? Why? Why? These actions are rooted in our self-identities led by ego, which is hooked onto a man-made concept called the Devil. The good side is that we are training our minds to cope with adversity. We need to develop the correct mental attitude to meet the challenges we will face in the future exploration of the Universe and beyond.

If life on Earth were purely "a bowl of cherries," we would not be mentally equipped to deal with the challenges we have to face. We are perfecting the Hi-Tech equipment to take on our mission. We are also perfecting the right mental thought process to take us on our journey. Egos will go away and allow mankind to unite so we can begin our mission. All living matter on Earth has a purpose in the master plan.

Plants and fish that survive in the deep parts of the oceans have no light at all. These species will have their role to play. Trees and plants give oxygen; ways of transplanting them onto inhospitable planets will be found. Animals are at the top of the intelligence chain at the moment, and all animals will contribute to the eventual mission of a physical presence on all planets of the Universe. A new Noah's Ark will be built. It will be a lot different than the one in the Bible.

Where does this intelligence come from? Who taught the lion how to attack? Who taught the dolphins and whales how to communicate? Who taught the birds how to survive extremes of climate? Who taught the apes and monkeys how to live in a structured society?

The answer is *"Blue Wave Intelligence,"* which all creations access through their brain. Plants have their own method of plugging into the *"Blue Wave force field."* Who or what is the source of all intelligence? This goes back to the beginning of our Universe.

MANKIND DISCOVERS

*Many years ago early man was quite crude,
he had no clothes, it was not rude, he was no prude,
when it got cold, no tailors were on file,
he dreamt of a design, bear skins became the style,*

*Life was simple, sometimes cruel,
man needed some help, so he invented many a tool,
he made clay pots, to cook food for all his little tots,
he made his own laws, because there were no Cops.*

*He dwelt in caves, it was all the rage,
when he needed advice, he would consult a Sage,
there were no books to read, no deals to seal,
then one day, man discovered the wheel.*

*As man progressed, many ideas were sought,
inventions from ideas, intelligent minds caught,
mankind's progress would have come to naught,
but for Blue Wave signals, given to deep thought.*

M.L.

The Universe

There is no beginning and no end. What keeps our Universe in a continual flow? Let us start at a point in time. Ten billion years ago we had a Big Bang. Our Earth was formed from a great explosion and after five billion years of changing from gasses to solid matter, the Sun was formed and then the planets of our Solar System. Over the next four and a half billion years, Earth evolved to its present day existence.

The Big Bang was not the beginning of creation as scientists will learn. It was a "Little Bang" within a Universe that already existed.

Every ten to twenty billion years, new sections of the Universe explode into existence and continue the expansion process. What scientists call black holes, I call *"Golden Holes." They are vacuum cleaners of the Cosmos. They are the re-creators.*

A Sun lasts for approximately ten billion years. When it starts to burn out it will turn into a Super Nova – a very bright Star. This is its final "Swan Song." It is a dying swan. The *"Golden Hole"* sucks in all the Planets and the Sun. God does not want the Universe full of rubbish. Nothing is ever wasted in Cosmic Law.

The *"Golden Hole"* continues sucking in all that surrounds the burned out Sun. Within the *"Golden Hole"* matter turns back to gasses. The gasses expand within a confined space -- then bang, another part of the Universe is formed. The bangs are of differing velocity depending on how big the Solar System was that burned out. What a great system.

Now we ask the question. *What causes all this to be? What is God?*

GOD'S PLACE

A star is born, it looks towards the sky,
it has a beautiful smile, a twinkle in its eye,
a miracle of life, a husband and a wife,
mankind exists for joy, without a care or strife.

Stardust from space, creator of the human race,
continuing on a pace, no final curtain to face,
a walking Universe, majestic glory is our nurse,
no time to be adverse, never in reverse.

Humming of dark matter, radio waves that flatter,
a view from infra-red, a time that humans dread,
gravity on the run, burning out of sun,
soon the work is done, golden holes are fun.

Worm holes without a clock, white dwarfs run amok,
dimensions within a band, a link of the human strand,
'Cosmic Blue Waves' give a taste, of the secrets of outer space,
Spirit conducts the pace, we all live in God's Place.

M.L.

The Dark

Throughout the whole of space there is an *"invisible force field"*; scientists call it dark matter. Do we need to be afraid of the dark? When the lights go out, all kinds of thoughts run through our minds and we can become lost. We pile away secrets hiding them in dark shadows and hope they never see light of day. The cause of these secrets is society's ploy of imprisoning the mind to adhere to impossible, unnatural ways to live. Fear lives in the dark so if we understand the meaning of dark, fear can no longer live there. It will become homeless and dissipate.

Light travels one hundred and eighty thousand miles per second through dark matter. Dark covers all of space and inside dark is intelligent energy. All material molecules and atoms are formed from dark energy, turning physical and seen in light. When we can get a better understanding of dark energy, we will be able to travel billions of miles in an instant. We do that when we die but since no one has come back to physical form to tell us about it, we will not believe it is possible. Physicists and scientists need facts and figures before they can prove anything. But first, they must have a theory.

Everything comes from somewhere; light comes out from dark's cover. The energy of heat and light are essential for all life. Without dark there can be no physical. Light uses dark as a shield to protect the physical. Dark is what we can see. The forces of energy are invisible, therefore, that dimension within dark we cannot see.

Now here comes the big secret. Inside dark is invisible light. This dimension is inaccessible. This is the powerhouse of everything. *"Golden Holes"* are the entrance and exit of matter.

When matter has lost its energy and is exhausted, it returns to a *"Golden Hole."*

This is a brilliant dimension of light far stronger than our minds can envision. This is all invisible to any matter molecule. Surrounding this invisible light form is invisible dark energy. This has a cover of visible dark. When the moment is right, the *"Golden Hole"* shoots invisible light energy into dark energy. This causes a big bang exploding light and heat into visible space and forming matter.

The Sun is a product of invisible light. We need very Dark sunglasses to see it. The Sun's power is a tiny fraction of the power of invisible light. That is why this immense power needs to be covered in dark, for without dark no physical matter could exist.

The dark is our protector and no fear can be attached to a protector. With this correct way of thinking, how can we fear the dark? Death is our greatest fear and we will be enveloped in dark -- what magnificent bliss.

While we are alive we can experience divine bliss. Close our eyes, drift off to dark space, surround ourselves in silence, clear the mind of every thought and we will connect to God. This is our identity. This is who we are. This is Eternal. Heights of exulted sensation on infinite speed of joy.

THE SPEED OF DARK

*Cast a vote in the Cosmic election,
tune to the wise channel for your protection,
you have a choice, make your selection,
listen to your Soul to obtain perfection.*

*Blue Waves traveling from out of the D-ark,
informing wisdom's, telling where to embark,
traveling through life to a blissful departure,
avoiding the trap-falls of the minds torture.*

*Dark energy encompasses all of space,
infinite speeds a winner of every race,
alive and well only by dark's grace,
making Earth such a wondrous place.*

*Light travels slowly through dark's splendor,
a void of multitude intelligence, a time and speed sender,
answers to everything, enveloping all the rolls,
dark of God holding Holy Scrolls.*

M.L.

When we want to think deeply, we close our eyes to clear our mind and keep out distracting images in the light. Our subconscious is in the dark permanently and that is where all the answers are found. Dark is God's cover. Wise sages of the past put their thoughts given by God in GOD's-ARK. This is a simple explanation of everything.

We will use the power of the dark to transport us on our journey of the future. It has many different dimensions. It is *"pure intelligence." It is responsible for everything. It is everything. A "pure intelligence"* that conducts and organizes the whole of the Cosmos. We are a living example of the brilliance of God. God is a label we humans have given to this power.

Statues and idols were created to worship God. Religions worship God. Atheists fight with religion but still acknowledge the existence of a source of power. No one can deny that there must be a power source from which they derive. God is as good a word as any. It does not require worship.

It does require respect and it should not be abused. The energy of God in *"Spirit"* creates a force field of gravity to keep everything balanced and on the move. It is all very simple. We are bubbles within bubbles. Every few billion years we blow another bubble.

BLOWING BUBBLES

*The cosmic forces are forever blowing bubbles,
clusters of stars forming from space's muddles,
emptiness filled voids, creating dust from gas,
gravity fed passengers, traveling first class.*

*The beginning of time, Universes waiting to form,
a wondrous peace, billions of years of quiet calm,
glorious eruptions, Golden Hole starts to explode,
transforming invisibleness into a matter mode.*

*A bubble within a bubble within a bubble,
forever expanding without any trace trouble,
all types of intelligence that are never lost,
the organization of a master-minded Cosmos.*

*Intricate equations that boggle the mind,
looking for answers that are hard to find,
the source of energy that created mankind,
using our Soul will make the secrets unwind.*
M.L.

Now we have established that Earth is a *Chosen Planet*. How do we go about populating the hostile environment of distant planets? It is obvious that the distances are so immense that normal modes of transport, such as rocket ships, are out of the question. We are the Essence of our thoughts, therefore, we have to find a way to transfer our thought through light waves and onto other Planets.

We have to turn matter back to invisible matter, attach thought to an energy force yet to be discovered and have it manifest into visible matter when it reaches the destination. This is not as crazy as it sounds - we can already clone animals. It will not be long before we can see a thought, record it and play it back on a screen.

Scientists are developing robots able to withstand hostile environments that would not sustain a human. Within the next few years, we could be manufacturing robots more intelligent than humans. If we do not get a grip on the way we have conducted ourselves over the past five thousand years, maybe we will need to be ruled by machines that will not allow all the conditioned negativity. They will tame other planets as the dinosaurs tamed Earth.

Unless we start to focus on our mission and cut out all the conditioned nonsense, we could end the same way as the dinosaurs. They lasted two hundred million years. The way we are going, we may not last another hundred years. The global heating and acid rain is taking its toll on Earth. The weather patterns are changing. Our mission will be short lived if we do not act as a united people and protect our life-giving *Chosen Planet Earth*.

This book will help us transform to a *Spirit*-led force of divine bliss. It will take many years before all mankind changes. By our example, we will show how life should be lived.

TREASURES OF THE UNIVERSE

*Life is an adventure with Earth as a playground,
everywhere we look, treasures can be found,
a ruby in a rose, diamonds glistening in a lake,
minds filled with beauty in dreams or awake.*

*Spiritual beings in human form,
pearls in eyes, seeing tranquility and calm,
floating on emerald seas, golden oceans so vast,
silver vapors in the clouds, platinum breezes as the mast.*

*Every rock holds beauty in its vein,
every leaf a different color, no shape the same,
flowing shrubs bursting with a glowing love,
God sets the scene, everything is a hand in his glove.*

*All joined together one poem in a universe,
every breath of air, is worth a kings purse,
jewels of joy, bliss from pole to pole,
magnificent enchantment, in our Universe Soul.*
M.L.

A Pure Diamond

A beam of light shines down from deep space. Its beam connects to a diamond here on earth. The diamond is a human being, a specie chosen to receive and transmit intelligence. The diamond has many facets and each facet contains memories. In our role model, this diamond has fifty facets; each one containing two years of memory, so we have a life of one hundred years.

Everything that happens within that life span is stored inside this diamond. Each facet can contain two years of memory and this is stored as a feeling, as a sensation, as a positive or a negative. If the sensation that is stored is on the positive sensation there is love, joy, happiness, peace, contentment and varying levels of divine bliss.

On the negative theme are worry, anxiety, anger, jealousy hatred, fear and varying levels of doom and gloom. All are stored together in each facet and connect to a central core.

There is a front facet that lets the light in from above. However, some diamonds are not very pure and have many distortions, cloudiness and rubbish contained within; the light cannot penetrate to the core. All the other facets soak up more and more rubbish as its life goes on, making each facet cloudy and dim.

When we focus on the negative side of life, then we continue to dim our diamond. We all have a very fine clear facet to receive the lights when we are born. However, most of us start to dim and distort it as we pass to another facet. If we focus on the joy of life then all our facets remain clear. We can remain a bright sparkling diamond with magnificent color and clarity – a shining example and highly valued.

Now here comes the next stage of the process. At the back of the diamond is another large facet - this cannot be dimmed or clouded or distorted. It does not hold memory, it collects the memories from the center core and beams them back into deep space. The diamond has been used as a receiver of intelligent energies and processes the energy into a physical form of intelligent matter. It also invents and creates new forms of intelligence then beams that information back into a dimension of space.

This dimension we refer to as Heaven or Hell. It is a vast infinite place holding eternal information created by the human form of intelligence. This is our connection to God. It is our true form, the finite form of the diamond will eventually end as dust. It was merely a vessel used to process an energy force of invisible intelligence.

So here we are in our eternal dimension diamond. There are no labels or symbols, no names, no language -- only sensation and feelings of magnificent splendor, streams of joy, wisps of ecstatic happiness. Bliss energized to feelings so magnificent that the sensations we had on earth are magnified a billion fold – a trillion fold. What true divine bliss encompasses us on a journey of everlasting joy.

CRYSTAL MINDS

*A flash so bright, a fantasy of magical light,
a crystal mind, colorful visions in a prism of sheer delight,
a paradise of splendor, received from a majestic sender,
gems of a wisdom blender, thoughts from the invisible mender.*

*The savoring of life, a vision of time divine,
ecstasy released to climb, rising to sensations so fine,
the winds caress, the feelings so sublime,
days of endless joy, a breeze tasting like wine.*

*A sea of tranquility, a star for all to see,
the fragrance of frankincense and myrrh,
the exultation of the senses, the beauty that does appear,
a trip that ascends, into the highest gear.*

*Comfort and care, in foreverness so vast,
true success, in the moments that pass,
blissfulness at last, Holy points that amass.
Sky miles on an eternal journey, traveling First Class.*
M.L.

There is also the other side -- Hell. We made it on earth and it is now multiplied in the dimension of eternity we created on earth. We manufactured Hell by our negative man-made concept of the way to live.

We were given joy and clarity of mind. This is our diamond, we distorted its brilliance, clouded its clarity, dimmed its color. So instead of having an asset of value, which is admired, we are left with a diamond that is used as an industrial tool to polish other diamonds. That will be ego's role in Hell.

Ego will be there as a warning to others not to follow our misguided dullness. Ego-led people will remain the flim-flam rubbing rags of Hell, seeing all the brilliant lights of Heaven; and these are the *Spirit*-led people we laughed at while we were in physical form. The Devil-guided people see Spirit-guided people as "Mumbo jumbo" people.

Remember "He who laughs last, laughs best."

GLORY VISIONS

*Another day in paradise,
a piece of cake, we all get a slice,
listen to the beat, the sound of the drums,
don't leave it too late or we'll be left with crumbs.*

*So many gaps we have to bridge,
suspended in mid air, on the edge of a ridge,
contentment of style, negotiating a joyful pact,
solving the puzzles of how to react.*

*Gazing up at the mountain so steep,
trying to rise from out of the heap,
avoiding the traps, the abyss of the deep,
wondrous dreams, in the quite of peaceful sleep,*

*Facing each challenge, Spirit as Utopia's crutch,
waterfalls of pure bliss, streams from Gods touch,
pleasures of majestic nature, moments in dizzy splendor,
infinite glory visions of our Holy divine defender.*

M.L.

Even at this point in our lives, it is not too late to have facets of clarity and brilliance. Maybe many of our facets are clouded and dimmed; but if we have clarity in our remaining facets, this brilliance will shine through and allow the light from above to clear a path to the core. So when the time comes, it will allow our beam of light to shine back in space's dimensions of eternity.

We will have changed our facets to feel "Heavenly Bliss." There may be many skeptical people who read these words and disregard them or put off transforming into a positive mode. *Do you really want to gamble on eternity?* Do you want to take your chances and allow a few years of physical negative man-made conditioning to spoil your Eternal Bliss?

Even if all you read in this book turns out to be incorrect, what have you lost by releasing the chains of negativity? The only risk you take by allowing yourself to be "*Spiritual Essence*" is that you will *live in joy* and maybe criticized for your enjoyment by the closed-minded.

ALMIGHTY ON LINE

Throughout my life I have found,
diamonds set in gold lying all around,
each generation blooming, from seeds in the ground,
branches on every tree, where joy and happiness abound.

Beauty rests in the peace on Earth,
realizations of what we are really worth,
cells filled with magical atoms that we breath,
oh, what a magnificent tapestry we weave.

Feeling close to nature in every way,
inhale the fresh air as we embrace the day,
stretch to the sky and touch the stars,
releasing our thought to enhance Cosmic Laws.

An existence of harmony and bliss,
Old ideas of worry scratched from the list,
Lasting joy, embracing Souls that God kissed,
almighty on line, connections to clear the mist.

A sacred calling on a higher tone,
never being cut off, never feeling alone,
a welcome on the hillside, a greeting in the dale,
enjoy the new service, "Spirit's Soul Mail."
M.L.

The Subconscious Soul

How can we recondition our minds to allow the beauty of life to be our main focal point? Quite a tall order when we are led to believe that the information stored in our minds is correct. How can it not be correct when most people think along the same lines? We are taught to have good manners. We are taught to accept all the labels and symbols within a religion. We are taught there is a God watching over us, and we must worship and please him.

We see all the new gadgets, electrical appliances, new styles in clothes and we want our share. We are taught to compete with one another – it's fun in sport, but is it so much fun in business? Whatever happened to simply "just enjoying the day." Water cannot flow up stream. Why do we try to live our lives going against the flow of nature? Ambition and striving to meet our goals is quite all right, provided we are aware of our true purpose to exist. *We exist to be in joy.* Losing this focus leads to many ailments.

When life becomes unbalanced, chaos and riot follow. This can lead to revolutions; which overthrow governments, only to be replaced with different doctrines that change the balance of rich and poor. Nothing really changes. Just new rules and regulations that are ignored by people with power. The masses still suffer. No Government has perfected the correct balance to this date. Even in the most sophisticated countries, society is breaking down.

Religion no longer has the respect of the masses. Divorce is on the increase, crime is rife, and people are hooked on drugs and alcohol. Our world is on the edge of disaster if our course is not changed. Global warming is becoming a real threat to future generations. World leaders speak fine words, but no real progress is being made to address the situation. A fundamental change in thinking has to come soon.

THE ONE AND ONLY

Holy wars and battles in God's name,
slaughter of the innocent, missing the intangible flame,
religious doctrines, all quite insane,
lost generations, only the photos in the frame remain.

Arguments and fights, no one's right or wrong,
slicing into fragmented pieces, singing a Holy song,
the shame of mankind, eyes filled with sin,
excuses for murder, within a devout hymn.

Battlefield for salvation, killing God's creation,
shame and pity on the human nation,
proving a point, an evil fascination,
Bibles written in Hell, from the devil's imagination.

The one and only power, each person a brick in the tower,
united as one force, peace and a harmony will endorse,
we're all connected to a one Spirit source,
learn the lessons well, on a "Joy for Life" course.
M.L.

An ancient Chinese Curse is "Have an interesting life." If life is calm, peaceful, joyful and happy, most people tend to find it uninteresting and boring. Bad news sells and it makes life interesting -- wars, famine, cruelty, scandal, crime etc. This is the meaning of the Chinese Curse.

All humans throughout the world need to know it is time to lift the curse they give themselves. We must stop subscribing to the folly of an artificial, materialistic world. We smother our feeling with material substitutes, overeating, alcohol, smoking, power, greed, etc.

When disaster strikes, it knocks us off our feet. We are distraught and this gives us a little time to reflect. *What is the reason we exist; why have we found ourselves in this predicament?* If we continually allow ego to be our reference point, then we are sentencing ourselves to a lifetime of worries and woes. No matter what remedies we take, they will be short lived.

On occasions we might have a "bout of brilliance." Our Soul peeps through as our guide and helps us arrive at a successful decision. It is not long before ego returns and we go back to our ignorance of the power that has eternal wisdom.

WHEN ARE WE GOING TO LEARN

Rejoice at birth, what will be our destiny,
Priest or murderer, decisions made by forces we don't see,
we play our roles, who will direct,
love or hate, do we have the power to select.

Thousands of years of mayhem with construction,
building our ivory towers, followed by insane destruction,
where do our leaders thoughts come from,
dumb societies rely on a smart bomb.

Turning away from Universal Laws, we call a bore,
youths blow up schools, now our attentions soar,
a seven day wonder, what's it all about,
has our culture got it wrong, can there be a doubt.

There is only one answer, there can be no division,
all religions must unite, one God with one vision,
all Nations under one flag, mankind must make this provision,
all life's forces endorsing Spirit's mission.
M.L

When we are asked a question we have to come up with an answer. As we go through life, we are tested with many adverse happenings.

When ego is master, we dismiss the correct solutions and allow our bodies to take this onslaught of trouble, worry and woe. We do not allow our subconscious Soul the time of day. There are no substitutes to find the correct formula to a joy-filled life. Why live in misery if we don't need too?

Only an egotistical man-made imaginary entity such as ego would ignore power the Soul gives. Most of us only use the subconscious to store memories, which contain mostly misguided negative conditioning.

Once the negative thoughts have been planted, there is no escape from the memory. The conscious mind can delay the thoughts from coming through; but when we become weak, ill or close to death, then all the things we have stored away in our subconscious comes back to haunt us. Most of the time it is too late to do anything about these thoughts and we carry them to eternity.

NO TIME

I have a little job for you to do.
You'll have to wait I'm too busy to help you.
But it's only a little job it won't take you long.
Well maybe later, I must run along.

Hello it is I, have you done that little job yet?
Oh! I'm awfully sorry, it's the little things I forget.
Well it should be done, do you want me to show you how?
No! There is no need, I'm just too tired now.

A week has gone by, the job has not been done.
Sorry! I have not had the mind, I must lay in the sun.
Could you please begin, can you please find the time?
I really don't know what you want, it has no reason or rhyme.

Seventy years have gone "bye" now, I hear you cry,
What was it that you wanted my talents to apply?
I wanted you to sit in silence, to find True Bliss Divine,
Oh dear! What a loss!
The real joy of life should have been mine.

M.L.

We should not allow the Devil power over our mind. We cannot change the world, but we can change the way we live our lives. We need to follow our own mentor. *Spirit* must become our guide.

The subconscious mind is our link with our Soul and the Universe. The Soul is not local. It has no permanent resting place. It is a lodger in our mind and body for a given number of years. It has sensations and is a pure essence within thought. It is an electronic impulse of sorts. It is an energy that cannot disappear and exists in many dimensions. It observes all that we do.

Our conscious mind has to link into our subconscious, and through a process of awareness, we start to recognize true power that creates and evolves all matter and anti-matter. This power is far greater than any human can envision. When we acknowledge our Soul, we do not question its power. When we are part of the energy flow, we accept and enjoy all it has to offer us. It makes us understand life in a totally new aspect.

We find that this is our real identity.

UNCONDITIONED LOVE

*The crack of the whip, sarcasm on the heels nip,
the crass comments, from the cynics lip,
loud and obnoxious behavior, of a bigoted lout,
oblivious ignorance, conceit given a pout.*

*Annoyance turned to anger, a flame to make the blood boil,
repetitive arguments, dueling without a foil,
concealed weapons, aimed at the ones we love,
missing the joy, sent on the wings of a dove.*

*Time passes by, and we still moan and cry,
morose and sullen, the 'weight of the world' till we die,
double depression, life is a bitch,
drugs and alcohol, make poor companies rich.*

*A Soul filled with Spirit, is the only discovery,
humans can find, on the road to recovery,
pitch all the pills, receiving advise from above,
find joy and happiness, in natures unconditioned love.*
M.L.

Where does our information come from? Humans have only been on earth for three and a half million years. Today we have evolved into a highly intelligent animal. The information has been around forever. In ancient times when mankind was supposedly uncivilized, we communicated messages by banging drums or sending smoke signals. We could hear the drums though sound waves that would carry quite a distance.

Today we are perfecting easier ways of transmitting information like cell phones, computers etc. The wave bands we use are all invisible. The machines we have invented to carry these messages to our ears and eyes came though our thought process. This is also invisible. The wave bands humans use has been here forever. We did not invent them - we discovered them with our invisible thought.

The information to build the machines to carry these wave bands must have come from the same source as the wave bands themselves. That invisible intelligence is part of our true identity. Humans could not access the information four million years ago because the human physical matter was not around then. Other animals and life forms used the intelligence to help them survive.

Most of the life forms around four million years ago have ceased to exist today. They were not able to acquire enough intelligence to survive. Their brain capacity was not able to fully absorb the *"Cosmic Waves."* When used by humans we call them *"Blue Waves."*

We are gaining more intelligence each day; but if we misuse this intelligence, then we will destroy ourselves with a misuse of information, not a lack of it, as with previous life forms. We are on the threshold of an amazing new era. An era led by

Spirit, with information and intelligence. We have the power to enhance the Cosmos well into the next thousand years.

We must now start to learn to use Soul as a guide to greater achievement, resulting in greater joy. Everything must stem from joy. The sex act is the most enjoyable feeling in the physical sense known to humans. It has to be fantastically enjoyable otherwise we would stop doing it and we would all disappear. From an ecstatic sensation, we start the process of birth. The intelligence required to formulate this process has been planned by *Spirit*. We did not plan it.

So it is with the way we humans receive our information to progress. It is waiting for an intelligence form to use it in a visible material way. *In it's invisible form, it is just pure bliss; it creates and evolves continually, eternally, infinitely, without beginning or end.*

We are "slap bang" in the middle of all this power. Our subconscious mind has access to this power. When we use our senses as a path to our soul, we begin to feel connected to the wonders of God.

ALL SOULS

Where do the colors go,
within a fading rainbow,
how do we measure man's woes in piles,
what is the distance between all the s-mile-s.

Is the penny about to drop,
when will the cradle fall from the tree top,
tears trickle down as the branches lop,
when will worry and anxiety stop.

Who is directing our central control,
how do salmon guide their shoal,
what directs birds from pole to pole,
can we dig ourselves out of the hole.

Is there a light, to show us the way,
just watch a kitten and ball at play,
see the dog laugh, his tail wags away,
all Souls glow bright, with Spirits magic ray.
M.L.

Senses of the Soul

Imagine being born blind. Many people are born with impaired or total blindness. They rely on their other senses to connect with the world around them. Hearing, smell, tastes and touch become extremely sensitive; heightening the sensations to enjoy life's offerings in a simple, more feeling manner.

Books will help us visualize images. Music will send sensations of rhythm and harmony to greater heights. We have many examples of blind artists who have achieved great musical fame and delighted audiences with their talent. Having a disability of the senses enhances the other senses we possess.

Most people have all their senses but are too wrapped up in the every day events connected to materialistic gain that they lose sight of the sensations of the senses. Go to any restaurant and see people stuffing their faces with food. How many are really tasting what they eat? Most are talking about insignificant "tittle tattle" and losing their taste bud's message.

We may walk in the countryside or in a park and be taken by the beauty of nature, but it is a fleeting sensation. How many of us stop and sit to look at a flower's detail or observe the bee taking it's share of pollen? Or to watch the way the leaves on the tree blow in all directions, and to look closely at each leaf to see the intricate detail of beauty in each leaf?

Imagine you were blind at birth. Then after twenty years you woke up one morning and you could see for the first time. How magical everything would seem. How wondrous this most simple item; we could see ourselves for the very first time and know what a magnificent miracle we truly are.

Why would we want to fill our minds with the trivial nonsense of gossip and prejudice? Why be jealous of anybody else when we can see our true selves? The nonsense means just that. *No sense*. We do not use our senses when we allow our mind to be cluttered with man- made nonsense. Our senses are our Soul's connections of non-visible to physical. By denying our mind and body of our senses, we lose the connection to our Soul.

People in general whine and moan about trivial events -- a stained shirt, panic for a late appointment, a demand of perfection; attachments to an ornament, and when it is stolen or broken, we get upset. We detach our awareness to our senses and substitute it for our ego's attachment to physical objects and mental impressions of the identities that we have built. All this is living in a false world of physical imagination.

Devastation happens on a regular basis for all life forms. It could be a violent storm or earthquake, or an act of atrocity by a manic Political Leader, or the illness or death of a loved one. Unless we know who we really are, these devastations will have a profound effect on our ability to enjoy our life. Since the only reason we exist is to enjoy, we will have wasted our physical lives.

By dividing ourselves by different Religions, it takes us away from a feeling of oneness with our fellow humans and nurtures individualism. To take a group of people away from the *Spirit of God*, and make rules and regulations of confirming with an ideology, distances communities from one another. As the distance grows, one community will decide one day it will not tolerate the other community -- war and atrocities then begin. Humans cannot survive in different groups. History is littered with millions of dead corpses killed by a religious fanatic.

Truly *Spiritual* leaders should climb down from their pulpits and embrace their fellow man without ceremony or labels and start a *Spiritual* bonding; which will bring together all religions, countries and specie of life.

THE LAND WHERE SOULS PLAY

An awakening to dawn mist on the water,
flowing Spirit's streams to God's altar,
purifying essence whistles through the trees,
images of the sacred blowing in the breeze.

Flights of fancy from birds up high,
feathers of many colors filtering through the sky,
sun, moon and stars envelops Earth's dome,
we're all birds of a feather, finding our way home.

Spectacle of mesmerizing movements flashing in the mind,
melting pots of humans, secrets hard to find,
love all embracing whispers on the wind,
no physical presence, ecstasy from a light dimmed.

Gifts of joy enmeshed in music and dance,
visualizing images filtering in a trance,
warriors in a drumbeat at journeys end,
back to the womb of creation enmeshed in a substance blend.

Wondrous dreams in the stillness of the dark,
journey on uplifting voyages in paradise park,
thunder and lightening points the way,
a prelude to the land where Soul's play.
                                    M.L.

Ego's With Taboos

In my two other books, I identified ego and self-identity as the culprit that causes many of our ills. Instead of ego using us for its advantage, it brings misery. We are going to learn how to use our minds and bodies to our true advantage, and not allow our minds and bodies to abuse us. This is a whole new ball game.

When we are born we are given a label -- it is our name. We then build an image around that name. The image has a personality and a memory bank of actions. We then start to seek symbols of success which society adheres to. These symbols are products of material wealth. They include designer labels, cars, being seen in the "right places," and acting out certain rules for the "right effect." Life becomes artificial. It is a manufactured designer lifestyle, encouraged by fashion magazines, advertising media, newspapers and other artificial elements. Certain newspapers are particularly good at distorting and sensationalizing the truth.

Mankind has been doing the same things time and time again for thousands of years, and infidelity and moral judgements still hit the headlines and sell newspapers to a public hungry for scandal. What a waste of precious time.

THE MORALS OF MAN

From the beginning of time, man ruled a sexual state,
Adam had nothing to contemplate, a spare rib made Eve his mate,
Solomon was smart, but a thousand wives was not enough,
he fell head over heels with Sheba, when she strutted her stuff.

Samson's fate was sealed, by a cunning conniver,
his hairdresser, happened to be called Delilah,
King David was a poet and a scholar, but love he did lack,
then one day Beth Sheba, became the monkey on his back.

Tarzan was a swinger, apes filled his brain,
he became smart, when he met his Jane,
Anthony wanted power in his grasp,
then one day, he was smitten by Cleopatra's asp.

At the time it seemed so great, a playmate was a must,
the fuel in the loin, is propelled by desire and lust,
What chance has a man got, so why get all fussed,
eventually the piper must be paid,
then we'll all end up as dust.
M.L.

Concentrating on the nonsense of an artificial society does no good to anyone who lives it as reality. It is an unreal world within nature. It seldom leads to any lasting happiness. In fact, the presence of keeping up with this artificial lifestyle leads us to all manner of illnesses and stress putting us in an early grave. Even the most basic body functions have become a form of taboo leading to shame and guilt.

For example we all produce gas in our bodies. If we pass this gas though our mouth as a burp, we have to apologize for a natural function. If we do not, then we are anti-social and rude. If we pass wind through our rear-end in front of company then disaster has stuck. This is just a basic normal body movement, yet it causes embarrassment. Why?

If we ask someone what kind of underwear they are wearing, this will cause embarrassment. Just over a piece of cloth. If we get upset by the pettiness of these basics, then all the rest of society's conformities are really going to leave us with a messed-up mind.

It never ceases to amaze me how we can watch a person blown to pieces on American television, yet if they show a nude woman they black out the nipples and genitals. We are made to be ashamed of our own bodies.

The male and female form is a beautiful gift. When we put them together and make love, wonderful sensations lift us to ecstasy. Why deny such fabulous feelings? Why restrict a normal act of physical joy? We are meant to enjoy sex with a clear unrestricted mind.

A lot of people suffer from panic attacks brought on by this mass of taboos. A negative view of life has built into uncontrollable fear. Their heart rate becomes rapid. They sweat and tremble. They may become nauseous and get dizzy. They can even have trouble swallowing. These are real feelings coming from a mind attached to a misconcept of life. *We have allowed ourselves to be attached to an intravenous drip of toxic thought.*

Negativity starts out as small "Must Nots" and soon become large "Can Nots."

The build up of a negative personal identity takes a long time and once it is allowed to dominate our Soul, we are at the mercy of a "blinkered" Ego. Do we really need to keep this cycle going or is there a better way to enjoy all society and still keep our true identity?

We need to grab ego by the scruff of the neck, reshape it and then use it to enhance. We have to learn to be balanced and focused at all times; not to allow all the negativity and pettiness that surrounds us, that distracts us from the joy of the day.

When we face negative forces, we can use ego as a shield of defense. What a great shield it makes. Instead of destroying us, it enriches and protects. Our ego recognizes the ego in other people, and analyzes how to destroy the negative thoughts from the other person. It apprehends and dismantles negativity, then sends a message back to the person's ego that is attacking us. It tells it in no uncertain manner to take a hike. Ego has now become our shield, a protector. We have used a negative force for a positive outcome.

When someone tells us we should act more responsibly, our ego can make a joke as a response. We no longer feel guilt. *We have the ability to respond in a more caring and meaningful manner to all eventualities.* We find the attacking remarks will stop. The negative person might try various other ways to force a worry, anxiety, guilt or jealousy into our mind, but we are no longer in the clutches of the Devil.

A CHANGE OF VIEW

Disaster is going to strike, life is quite stark,
I have an idea, I'll build a Noah's Ark,
It's taken ten years to complete, there's no sign of rain,
as time progresses it seems my worries were in vein.

What a nice day, I'll go for a sail,
before it was lunch I was swallowed by a whale,
it was quite dark, my Spirit became a-light,
I was blown out, there was no need of a flight.

I complain a lot, I don't believe there's a God up above,
I can't even afford to buy a new glove,
my views changed when one day I saw a Marching Band,
a young boy was clapping although he had no hand.

Life's not fair, why can't I be rich,
I have a shovel and I keep digging my own ditch,
my views changed when I saw the terminally ill,
now every day my Soul gives me a happiness pill.
M.L.

Our awareness is using our Ego to protect us. Prejudice and bigoted views will never interfere with our view of peace and harmony. Our ego has relinquished our self-identity to materialism and sent love and joy from our Soul to the negative person.

No more defending a point of view. No more arguments. Life becomes far more peaceful.

Ego has joined Soul and now they act as a team. United we stand, divided we fall. We see people all around floundering, by not using ego correctly and allowing their ego's to abuse them. By our example, they will pick themselves up and join the club called *E-goes, Soul Shows*.

We then find we attract like-minded people who want to help us achieve all the wonders life has to offer. They become our sentinels and we theirs. Pretty soon we have a whole band of sentinels. We are getting success in life and no effort is required. Life is beautiful.

LIFE IS BEAUTIFUL

Projected visions in a pain of glass,
shattered lives that did not last,
memories of dread, appear in a frame from a forgotten past,
all the lost hours of worries that amass.

Eons of winters, no sign of warm,
always stormy seas, never seeing calm,
counting dollars and cents, blinded to flowers bloom,
piling up green crinkly paper in the garden of doom.

Swings of moody shows, anguish of lingering doubts,
fighting with unknown foes, wrestling anxiety bouts,
shouts of peace and quiet, whisperings from a distant source,
mighty strong messages from the Eternal Power Force.

Soaring higher than an eagle, eyes in Spirits focus,
breaking free from evil's hocus Pocus,
minds waking up, senses taking notice,
Life is Beautiful, immersed in Souls healing poultice.
                                                            M.L.

True Values

I know this man who is ninety-one years of age. He is a happy man and always has a smile on his face. He has all his faculties. One day I asked him "What do you put your longevity down too?" I thought he was going to say plenty of exercise and good wholesome food, but he didn't. Instead he replied, "The man upstairs has been so busy he forgot about me!" We all need humor like this to take us through our day.

He can remember being two years old and running between his father's legs while he was shaving. His father picked him up and put him outside the bathroom. Such an ordinary event, yet eighty-nine years has passed by and it seems like yesterday that his father removed him from the bathroom.

"Time goes by so fast," he said to me this morning; and now while I write these words in this book, a ninety-one year man awaits his passing and clings to every second. Ninety-one years seems a long time when we are young, but it passes in a blink.

MY SPIRIT'S VOICE

I awoke one morning and I was old,
where did time go and the memories I hold,
I missed so much, places missed and yet,
I really can't say I have any regret.

My vision caught by a dimming past,
when I was young I thought forever I would last,
now as the fingers on the clock whizz by so fast,
I realize the darkness my shadows cast.

At ninety-one the moment means so much,
I long for the loved ones I have touched,
why did I fuss when I played out my role,
lucky for me I followed my Soul.

If I had my time over again, what would I change,
not a thing, I suppose that seems strange,
I made many a mistake, I learnt quick by God,
I know all too soon, my body will lie under the sod.

My physical form means little to me.
All the wrinkles and creases will soon be let free,
I should be sad, instead I rejoice,
for I have always been in tune with my Spirit's voice.

M.L.

Oscar Wilde said "Youth is wasted on the young." None of us must waste a second; learn from our elders that every second is precious and we must enjoy the moments. We can all remember back to early childhood, and as the years fly by, we begin to realize what is important to us. The sooner we learn the true lessons of life, the better our remaining years become.

Nobody knows when he or she is going to die. When we are in our teens we give no thought of getting old and dying. As the years pass by and our ambitions do not come to fruition, we become disappointed and sullen. *We have a list of "If Only's." If only I would have done this. If only I hadn't done that.*

With hindsight we could have all progressed better. Dwelling on past memories manifests into a never-ending circle of self-defeating thought. Mountains build out of molehills. Grudges and remorse flood the cells in our brain. We have snookered ourselves into a position of living hell. This condition has taken all our lives to build; how can we reconstruct a "Gerry-built" brain. First, look into the mirror five times a day. When we are in thought, just walk over to the nearest mirror and take a look at the expression in our face. Would we like to look at that all day long?

What we see in the mirror is what we feel inside our body. This is how other people are seeing us. Are we bringing joy into their lives by our facial expressions. If we see a happy smiling face in the mirror then our thoughts are on the correct channel. Most of us are not.

Just go for a walk and see how many smiling faces there are around you. Even people who have all the money they could desire and have a "good lifestyle" by society's standards, still look miserable. What has gone wrong?

When we have a photograph taken we all smile. Why wait for a photograph? When we bring out the family album we see all smiling faces, this is how we want to feel but it should not be forced. No one should have to tell us to "smile please."

We are being recorded every second of our lives by the camera in the heavens. This is the real candid camera, no tricks. It will be played back many times in the timeless program of eternity. What part you end up with depends how well you have rehearsed your lines. To be a shining star, we must rehearse well. Our lines are all ad-lib.

We can say and do what we please, our roles here on Earth are magnified a trillion times within the infinity of the Eternal Flow within dimensions of sensations. A projected image of light with no tangible matter, similar to light shining through a roll of film. Do we want to be a positive or a negative, black and white, or color?

Smile Please, This is the Real Candid Camera

We must have a new measurement of wealth. What is our most pleasurable gift we possess while we are on earth? *It is "time."* We must learn to spend it wisely. Every second is like a million dollars. So we are wealthy beyond our wildest dreams. If we invest in joy, then every second spent has earned us interest, compounded again and again.

A gain. No loss. Lost money can be recouped, losing seconds cannot. Every second is a treasure of bliss. Squandering them is mankind's folly. It doesn't matter whether we are intellectual or academic, a professional, a business "whizzkid," housewife, child, whatever, every second counts. We cannot recoup the lost seconds. We can learn how to nestle in an abundance of joy. We have to allow a power-source that is ever present to be our guide. We have a free will.

No one can affect our Soul, only our own mind. The electrical power that comes into our home can be directed to a light or television where we control the switches. Our minds have the ability to switch on a light, which is our source of bliss. One hour of meditation a day will start a new thought process.

Releasing past memories is the first step to switching on the light. We then have to release our attachments to all materialistic things, including our body. Then we must release our attachment to nature, to the flowers, the trees, the sun, moon, stars. All physical attachments must be relinquished before we can find divine bliss.

When we learn to meditate with a clear mind with no thought whatsoever, we begin to release our attachments to the physical world and connect to the infinite world.

We can then return to the physical world and link to nature in a joyful, uncluttered way. We have come full circle back to **babyhood**. (If this word does not exist, then it has just been born.) This time we have the maturity of the world with *Spirit* as our guide.

We can plan our future in any way we desire in the comfort and security of being enveloped in a magical force of supreme bliss, which is our Eternal Force of everything that has infinite might. From this point in our mind we can reach out and touch the whole of the Universe. Our Planet with its fusion of magnificent beauty has abundance for us to enjoy.

Every morning when we awaken we can look forward to seeing, hearing, feeling, touching, smiling all the beauty that exists. What a wonderful world -- full of ecstatic wonders.

What treasures are we to seek today?

FRUITFUL LIFE

The enchanted garden, seeds planted by God,
growing in paradise, peas in his pod,
succulent tastes, every second is a peach,
joy abounds, we only have to reach.

Glory infused vegetation, abundance exists in every nation,
savoring the juices, what a wonderful intoxication,
happiness stemming on the branches of the fruitful,
life is a plus, in the eye of the pupil.

Don't be misguided by attachment to the unreal,
harshness in thick skins, allow negativity to peel,
strip to the core, let our golden roots reveal,
salad days of plenty, Spirit makes a blissful meal.

The perfumed breath of the orchids flame,
hand in hand, Souls floating down Lovers Lane,
tumbleweed blowing in the prairie and on the plain,
tingling freshness, crystal drops of rain.
M.L.

Shopping Basket

Once upon our time there was a young boy growing up in a poor neighborhood in a far away land. He was two and a half years of age and had seven brothers and sisters. His mother was a religious person who suffered with arthritis and had difficulty walking. Every day he would watch his mother go down on her knees and pray to God. She would pray to help overcome her pain and to help with their poverty. Each day the children had to help her back on her feet after her prayer.

The young boy never saw any improvement in their plight. The more his mother prayed the worse her condition became. This went on for twelve years. At the end of this time his mother died at a young age. This event had a remarkable effect on the fourteen-year-old boy.

When the family went to church he noticed a basket would be passed around to collect money. Although the congregation was poor, all the people contributed and put money in the basket.

The boy left school at an early age and moved from job to job. When he reached his nineteenth birthday, he had an amazing thought. "I am going to invent my own God and my own church. Unlike the religious God, my God is going to distribute food and I am going to give a basket for people to put food in. I need to do this at a faster pace than the church so to speed things up it will be a basket with wheels. People will put food in it and wheel it around a store." In this world we make our own luck. If we have to invent a God it is quite all right provided we live by *Spirit's* guidance. *God helps those that help themselves.*

TOUGH LUCK

Some people are far from the mark,
seeing life as some kind of lark,
all of a sudden, they have a big fall,
if they didn't have bad luck, they'd have no luck at all.

Luck be a Lady To-night,
why does life have to be such a fight,
a throw of the dice, a spin of the wheel,
some people are lucky, if they even get a meal.

Round it goes, when it stops, no one knows,
life is good, if we can take the blows,
working too hard, may make us frazzle,
all we needed, was a little mazel.

They say where there's money there must be muck,
in life we make our own luck,
the secret of luck is leave nothing owing,
when the going gets tough, the tough get going.
M.L.

With his God's help and his belief, he became a multi-millionaire. He turned an adverse start in life into a financial success. He was happy to do this work; in fact it was not work, it was his religion which he believed in. He knew it could not fail. He is now in his seventy's and all he wants is health and time. He possesses joy.

He is not aware that his joy is his *Spirit,* and in reality, his God is the same God as religions, the same God as Atheism, and the same God as Agnostics. There is only one source of power for everything, man-made or nature made, Solar System made or Cosmos made. If we allow ourselves to open to God then every success we can envision will come to us.

If we allow worries, fear and anxiety to rule our minds and then pray for help, it will not come. We have to dismiss negativity from our mind, be thankful for being alive. That is enough. Just being on this planet, being able to see the beauty of nature is enough. If we have pain be thankful we are alive to feel the pain; embrace it, it will disappear far quicker than if we allow self-pity to overcome our brain. *Life is meant to be enjoyed; balance and focus on what we have, not on what we don't have.*

Look at people who have achieved with pride as a member of the same club. The Human Race Club. We are all the same -- white, black, yellow, British, Chinese, American, French, Australian, Jew, Christian, Buddhist, Hindu, Atheist, Agnostic. It does not matter. *We all exist to enjoy our existence. We are all one.*

The same power source drives all our motors. Whether one wants to acknowledge that power is up to the individual person. The people that use ego flounder through life with no true purpose. No matter what material wealth or high position they achieve, they will not find the real joy they were meant to have.

We must not wait to find the source of joy. Every day we must fill our baskets with joy. This makes us wealthy beyond compare. If any religion breeds hatred, then God has no part in that religion. That is a man-made mockery of God.

The devil that rules religions will increase our fear and anxiety. No true *Spiritual* leader would preach Hell and damnation. Their minds are conditioned by negative-based assumptions of the identity of man. They see only the human form and not the true everlasting Essence that is inside man. The finite physical man is only a shell being controlled by Ego or Soul.

The preacher that attacks the ego has to have ego himself. The preacher who enhances *Spirit* has *Spirit* himself. Evil and bad are a man-made condition. If we do not recognize them they cannot exist. If we concentrate on our true identity there would be no need of any laws of any kind.

A true flowing Eternal Essence has no restriction or boundaries. Only ego-led humans need rules and regulations to keep them in order. Early man did not need them for they were led by their *Spiritual Essence,* and the fact that we are here today means it worked very well.

DISTORTION OF FAITH

A gentle man, eating humble pie,
days of worship, eye in the sky,
frivolous pursuits, senses begin to dim,
preacher to the cows, milking humans taking vows.

Prices on the rise, ceremonial treasure of size,
confessions of lies, no one hears the cries,
possibility of thought, denominations to be caught,
circles of hope on files, missing God by miles.

Accentuate the split, religions filled with grit,
rules and regulations live, drained through a sieve,
monuments of great divide, splitting humans on every side,
Holy Wars to fight, blind faith with spite.

The lies on behalf of God, hatred under the sod,
amassing wealth from the poor, devil knocking on the door,
crosses turn to swords, battles of the hordes,
total abuse of power, death by the hour.

Fan the flames of hate, man's religions create,
a mockery of truth, time to raise the roof,
all unite as one, divisions slowly gone,
Spirit gives the nod, we are a little child of God.
                                              M.L.

The image of God is different for many people. I was at a party and met a charming elderly couple. This couple is homey, salt-of-the-earth, wonderful human beings. I asked the lady how she perceived God. After a little deliberation she said "most people see God as a man with a long beard but I see him like a Roman Centurion, standing by a large rock."

My friend, who supplies Drug Stores with all manners of toiletries asked, "Is this Roman clean shaven?" and she replied "Yes." He then asked, "Can you let me know who supplies his razor blades? I would like the order - what a great advertisement that would make."

Having an image of God in our mind is fine and if that image brings comfort, it is something you can become attached to. *You can never be disappointed as long as you don't expect any favors. God helps those that help themselves.* Of course this is only a man-made image and when we see it on a deeper level, we transfer man's image of God into a pure *Spiritual Essence*.

God can be all things to all people. What we must not do is allow other people or any man-made concept to become our God in the true sense.

I remember back in Manchester, England, people idolized their soccer teams and probably still do today. If Manchester United lost their match, I know some people who would not eat their dinner that evening. All the next week would be enmeshed in a sad feeling until the following week's match. It is the same with the stock market. Some people's moods depend on whether their stocks go up or down; their feelings follow the gyrations.

People also idolize other people. Princess Diana was a role model for many people and when she was killed in a car crash, the whole world was devastated. In the United Kingdom, a whole week was dedicated to mourning. People openly wept at the departure of their icon.

REMAIN A BRIGHT LIGHT

A star is born, privacy gone astray,
the leading lights, far too soon fade away,
the devil makes sure, the good don't stay,
the forces of darkness, dictate the state of play.

Princess Diana made us all cry,
the devil's henchmen hound and pry,
she was a Good Angel, her love she did apply,
evil struck and made the Princess die.

Margaret Thatcher was a great leader,
she had honor and truth, integrity did feed her,
she fought evil face on, she would not crack,
then her own party, stabbed her in the back.

In our lifetime, we all rise and fall,
the moment of truth, when our backs are to the wall,
we will NEVER pay the devil his due,
with Spirit's help, our strength will renew.

M.L.

We all have attachments to many things, people, teams, money, family, friends; this is a part of living. However, a strong attachment to our Soul will not allow a distortion, hysteria, or mania to invade our joy of life.

Concern and care for others are always a priority; but God is our *Spiritual* being, our attachment, our icon, our guiding force. We must never let human events distract us away from the divine bliss we all deserve to live in.

Put one hundred people in a room and ask, "Who is God?" and we will probably receive one hundred different views. Religions divide God by using different customs and symbols to show the route to God's ears. The mistake all religions make is viewing God in human terms.

In the Bible it says "God made man in his own image." That was written by a man. That passage was not meant to be taken in the physical sense. We are made in God's image in the *Spiritual* sense. Our energy source is our Soul. It has no shape or form but is God's image.

When a man like Jesus came along he epitomized what God would be if we could see a Soul. He was a man of pure joy and love, and preached goodness all his life. Jesus was not meant to be idolized. God has no physical form and to just see God as a human is like looking at a wonderful painting of a landscape and seeing one brush stroke.

The whole of the Cosmos is filled with God. It is an energy of intelligence with trillions of dimensions. Humans are a dimension of physical life that has access to a few of the dimensions of intelligence. We are part of the whole, complete and incomplete at the same time; drops of water, yet when connected form an ocean.

Division on God allows the man-made images to become paramount in our mind. It replaces God with physical substitutes and these substitutes lead to arguments, fights and wars. It also conditions our mind to feel guilt and hatred. We don't live up to the standards of the Rules and Regulations.

Knowing and understanding how our Soul can connect our physical mind and body to God is the only route to a joyful, loving life without worry and anxiety. By keeping life simple, we should see God in every blade of grass, every tree, every mountain, in the wind, in our voice, eyes, touch, smell and hearing.

This tunes our thoughts to God. The message we receive will take us through life in joy and love, no matter what physical devastation comes our way.

Be a Spring

Imagine we are a spring, we are very bouncy and we can jump to great heights of joy. When we face a negative situation we feel pressure on us, we feel squeezed. We begin to feel compressed. We start to sink lower and lower. As the situation worsens we feel more pressure and we coil into ourselves. We now feel very small indeed.

The world has attacked us and we have compressed ourselves into a powerful coil that at the correct moment will be released. Something happens then we release the catch.

"TWANG." Up we jump to a great height of exultation.

A LONG-TERM INVESTOR

A long-term investor in the Cosmic Trust,
a Mutual Bond that cannot go bust,
an Insurance Policy that is a must,
no withdrawals, no clatter or fuss.

We deposit our Souls on an eternal ride,
filtering streams full of Universal pride,
a place where worry and fear can't hide,
joyful bliss with God at our side.

Ecstatic exultations faster than light,
visiting stars that are out of sight,
fascinating journeys with infinite height,
all propelled by the glory of Spirit's might.

A flight without wings, bouncing on everlasting springs,
floating on the notes that guardian angels sing,
a constant rainbow, profusion of joy that color brings,
Savoring the fruits of love, happiness & harmony
in all things.

M.L.

We allowed a negative situation to give us great power. Now we are jumping all over the place; fantastic energy abounds. We have exerted great strength from something that should have laid us low for a long time. Instead we gave the negative situation a little time to recharge our coil and just when we thought it was getting the better of us we blossomed into a new season. We are like a newborn lamb.

Spring is the beginning of a joyful summer season. We can now become a mountain spring, sparkling, glistening, gleaming - *A clear pure flowing Essence of energy. A spring aspiring into a season, into a stream.* We have become a magician. We have magical power and we are "SPiRitING" all through our lives. *SPIRIT* is our spring.

When we bounce, our ego gets trounced, we enjoy our lives to the last ounce. An eternal spring with a constant flow, we feel our Soul, as we feel the wind blow.

Negative Junkie

There is a large section of society who live in a negative mode throughout their lives. They feel comfortable in this mode, and on the rare occasions, they put their guard down and allow joy to come into their lives. After a while, something comes along and shocks them back into the negative mode.

This takes them lower than they were before joy was felt. When this continues to happen they become frightened to show joy because they know it is going to be taken away, so they stay in a negative mode throughout their lives.

By attaching our thoughts to the materialistic world, we lose track of real joy. We become embroiled in gossip and tittle-tattle. We immerse ourselves in negative talk. We read negative news. When we show joy there is always someone around to try and take the smile off our face. We are indoctrinated to look miserable. Look around, watch people driving their cars. Look at the faces of the people on the sidewalk. How many smiling faces do you see? The worries of the world are on everyone's shoulders.

MARTYRS TO WORRY

*Martyrs to worry, always in a hurry,
don't think life is funny, need a lot more money,
like to water weeds, like to dig up seeds,
too bored with the hours, no time to smell the flowers.*

*Answers 'no' when joy is sought, frightening thoughts are caught,
anxiety comes to naught, happiness cannot be bought,
a conditioned mind, taught by society's course,
building up worry, hiding in a Trojan Horse.*

*Need to reload, ammunition for a depressed mode,
combinations to anxiety code, the key to the hatred road,
secrets to keep, turbulent waters run deep,
moments of joy take a peep, jealousies make them seep.*

*Time is of the essence, negativity has no sense,
use the senses to be aware, life was meant to be without a care,
start to climb our blissful stair, begin to use our creative flair,
in Spirit we inspire, each day a level divine,
journeying higher & higher.*

M.L.

What a sad position people have allowed himself or herself to be encased in. *They have become negative junkies.* They are hooked on the down side of life. It matters not whether they are affluent or not. In fact, the more affluent they are the more miserable they become.

POOR LITTLE RICH GIRL

Shooting poisoned darts from minds filled with hate,
being caught up with our own self-satisfying bait,
lives of toxic thought, never finding a true loving mate,
missing our ship of dreams, death's certainty will not wait.

Entangled lives immersed in trouble and worry,
running to another anxiety, in a frenzied hurry,
longing for the love, a child gives a mother,
a fading existence, believing we were borne to suffer.

A life covered with money and fame,
no substance or joy, emptiness and frustration enriching the pain,
a myriad of tunnels leading to a void in an unreal world,
a labyrinth of depression and foreboding, all twisted and curled.
M.L.

How do we kick the habit? First of all, recognize it -- we were not meant to live this way. People are always running to the doctor. I'm sick doctor, help me. The doctor will not be able to help himself unless he recognizes his own *Spiritual Essence*. If he is conditioned the same as his patients, it is only a matter of time before he is running to his doctor. *We were not meant to be sick. We were not meant to be unhappy. Most sickness is manifested from negative minds.*

Each derogatory comment we make is a nail in our own coffin. It builds toxin in our system. Taking anti-depressant tablets is not going to solve the problem. It will only mask the symptoms for a short while. We move from hooked on negativity to being dependent on pills.

The next stage is to be dependent on the surgeon. The next stage is making sure we have a burial plot -- one with a good view. All because we have been trained to think in negative terms.

We need to start to study ourselves. See how many non-positive words we speak in a day, record ourselves, make notes. Most of us do not realize how negative we have become. Only when we start to recognize how we are programmed we can move on to the next step of self-improvement. The newspapers continue to focus on bad news. They seem to take delight in a person's downfall.

BOOMERANG

*The coupe is in the scoop,
never allow the news to droop,
dig the dirt, how low can you stoop,
be careful not to rub your nose in the poop.*

*News at any cost, never mind the loss,
no privacy for the famous, media is the boss,
nibbled to the bone, loves to cast the first stone,
persistent pursuits are prone, never left alone.*

*Continual ring of the phone, till the mind is blown,
seeds of hate are sown, no will to atone,
sensational news to create, splitting a man from his mate,
public thirst for a broken state, morals to contemplate.*

*Gossip and scandal to mingle, makes the brain start to tingle,
then one day, holy gee! The media is after thee,
run as you may, you'll never get free,
the monster you created,
will be your own downfall La! De! Dee!.*
M.L.

Wouldn't it be wonderful if a leading newspaper would have the sense to only report on man's miraculous creative ability for a week. Keep all the doom and gloom in small print in the back section of the newspaper and use all the headlines to promote mankind's miraculous joy and inventiveness.

Write about all the new talent. Promote all the new musicians, artists, poets and philosophers. A week of positive reporting will have a dramatic effect on all the readers. The week will turn to a month, then a year. Then there is no going back. Making news all positive. Keep the negative stuff in small print in the back. Other newspapers will see the success and they follow.

All of a sudden we will have a transformation of the media. Now they are going out looking for good news. The way to hit the headlines is to become positive, so now more people become achievers; that is the way to attract attention and to become successful.

By our example of not subscribing to any newspaper or media negativity, we can play our part in the remodeling of our society.

No Hopers

There are many people who have tried to achieve their goals and have failed. They have given up and live in despair. Every time they tried they met a wall of negativity. People telling them their work was no good or their timing was not right, and many more excuses why they did not want to be involved.

If we enjoy what we are doing then it makes no difference what people say or do, we continue our enjoyment and find new and more creative ways to express ourselves. Maybe our work isn't that great at the moment, but if we continually improve our thought process we will achieve our dreams.

What about all the people who are stuck in 'DEAD END' jobs? What about people who are in constant pain or the sick and dying? These people really see no future and the deeper their despair, the sicker they become. No physical or material substance in the whole Universe is permanent. *Everything evolves then erodes.*

Our Planet is constantly on the move. Tectonic platelets beneath the surface are constantly shifting. Mount Everest grows a little every year. The whole of the surface of the Earth will change in the course of time; eventually the Earth will disappear along with the Sun and Moon and all our Solar System. Every Star and Planet will disappear in the course of time. New Planets will form, new Solar Systems will form, and new intelligent life forms will form.

DREAMS OF HOPE

*How do we cope,
living in the land with no hope,
we could wash away our troubles of mope,
if only we would find the magical soap.*

*How can we deal,
with fear that makes our fate seal?
Why gamble on the way that we feel?
Why keep our hand on hold, waiting for the winning deal?*

*Why do bad things happen to you and me?
Our eyes are open, but we cannot see,
what does it mean to feel truly free?
Oh! for the chance to sway like a tree.*

*How do we manifest the joys of our dreams?
How do we rid the tears of a lifetime of screams?
Nothing is ever as bad as it seems,
let's be guided by our Soul, then see how our face beams.*
M.L.

We humans are part of the system. We must not get bogged down with self-pity because we are not as healthy or successful as we would like to be. We are on the surface of Earth, we are alive and we dwell in the Garden of Eden.

Earth is the Garden of Eden.

Beauty abounds in every direction. We have lost our focus and only see what our conditioned ego mind wants us to see. The mold has to be broken. We are not a permanent fixture and nothing is in the physical. In *Spirit* nothing is ever lost.

The whole of the Universe can disappear in the physical form, but it only goes back to its home from where it came. *We are visiting the physical world along with the mountains, the seas, the plants and all matter.* Just visitors for a short period of time; why waste the time on despair when there is nothing to despair over. If no one or nothing is here forever, then our focus is to enjoy this moment. That is all we possess. Moments in time.

EVERYTHING

Music on the winds of time,
strings of accord, tunes quite fine,
seedlings blown on a course divine,
notes in key, serenity of heart and Soul sublime,

Distant horizons held in our hand,
amazing compositions in a grain of sand,
unfettered love, harmonious perfumed scent,
floating without form, complete abandonment.

Zodiac signs, future twinkles from a far,
making a wish on a shooting star,
Leo and Virgo fishing in eternity,
catching a Celestial storm with Libra and Pisces.

Wisdom of the wise, eyes glaze the Cosmic window,
Heavens above, Heavens below, all around an everlasting flow,
sparklers of the Universe, saturated space, Spirit does inspire,
Joie de Vie in brilliant color, everything, all energies can desire.

M.L.

In a few moments we may not have the physical form to enjoy. No human can control the time they have on Earth. *This moment is precious and we must not let it slip by without savoring its exquisite delights.*

All are free and ours to see, smell, feel, hear and taste. Go to a beach, open our mouths, let the wind blow the salt air on to our tongue. Go to the countryside smell the flowers and plants. Feel the texture of a rose petal, the bark of a tree, they are a part of us. Listen to the birds sing their songs of joy. Open our eyes to the Moon and Stars at night. Immerse in the delights of the night.

THE SHOW OF THE SEASON

Cast a shadow on the rippling ocean,
moonbeam waving in a flow of motion,
a roaring silence, a soothing commotion,
a delightful formula, a brilliant notion.

Twinkle, twinkle, Venus loves from a distance far,
Celestial visions emerge, God sparks a shining star,
Earthly beings entranced in a wink,
enraptured in a chain, enhanced as a link.

Ships that pass in the still of the night,
a descending hush, then a blinding flash of light,
electric fireworks illuminate the sky,
a call for drums, thunderbolts reply.

The show of the season, no tickets are needed,
all well rehearsed, when the plans were seeded,
produced and directed by magical intelligence,
exaltations of the real, sensations for our sense.
                                                M.L.

A Positive and Negative Balance

Electric current needs a positive and negative to flow. Humans need the same. However, we need ten units of positive for one unit of negativity. Too much negativity and we overload. We fight with each other or get sick through mental anguish; then we disappear before we should.

Too many positives and we can also blow a fuse. Being too successful in the material world makes us a slave to our work or artistry. Look at Mozart, he burnt himself out at an early age. His brilliance did not help him survive to old age. Many very rich people who have injured their health through the stress and strain of the business world would give up all their riches to regain their health.

THE GRAVY TRAIN

Take a ride, on the Gravy Train,
clickety clack, on the track to no gain,
wealth and fortunes, to a destination with no name,
no signals to stop, forgetting the station,
from whence we came.

The journey of a lifetime, seeing love in money,
hands in the pots, grabbing all the honey,
no time to taste the sweetness, collecting all the jars,
blinded to the sidings, filled with rusty cars.

Looking out the window, see the years whizzing by,
still stoking up the furnace, driven to be the fastest to fly,
racing with all the locos, missing all of natures beautiful shows,
messengers with no message, answers only the devil knows.

Coming to the end of the track, alas no brakes,
crashing into oblivion, ego is all it takes,
all the wealth piled high, smoldering in a heap,
going round in circles, in the abyss of the deep,
mankind begins to weep.

If only love can be found, but where do we look,
born in happiness, then consumed in misery, because fate overtook,
bliss is waiting quiet and still, for us to switch on the power,
time to use our own free will, arriving on Spirit's hour.

M.L.

We can never overload on joy. Every day we need to increase our joy, which in turn increases our love. This fuels contentment and simplicity, which also keeps our bodies healthy. Joy uses the forces of positive and negative purely as the energy flow it was meant to be.

Joy and love are transmitted from our Soul – it is our link to the whole of the Cosmos. The Cosmos is God or whatever name gives us understanding of its infinite Eternal Power. Who can ever feel hopelessness or despair when all this creation is here for us to savor?

GOD'S REAL COOL

God without religion,
God without condition,
God gives us all vision.
God makes us make the right decision.

God gives infinite possibility.
God makes our minds free.
God wakes us up with joy and glee.
God makes us smart, with plenty of ability.

God makes us real cool.
God allows us to be nobody's fool.
God says love ourselves, we are a jewel.
God says enjoy life, it's the Golden Rule.

God is the 'one' we all thank.
God is the 'one' we turn to when our plan sank.
God turns our minds into a think tank.
God says sometimes, our brains need a yank.

God says look in the mirror and see.
God says you are all part of me.
God says you are a miracle of life, golly gee.
God says health, wealth and gladness will be for thee.

God takes us into the Cosmic Flow.
God makes us high when we feel low.
God takes us through life with a Ho! Ho! Ho!
God gives balance and focus, stops us being a Yo Yo.

M.L

The Town Crier. Oh Yay! Oh Yay! Oh Yay!

We all know someone who's philosophy of life is 'you have to worry' if you are concerned about anyone. That person goes around visiting people who are in pain or have a problem and take their worry with them. They continually focus on the sad side of life; and although their loved ones may have died many years ago, they will continue to cry over them on a regular basis. When events come along that need comfort and advice they inflict more sadness into the situation.

They watch soap operas on television; this is a good training ground to condition the mind into sadness and tears. Their mind is now conditioned to cry at the drop of a hat. Many people find themselves in this situation and do not realize how trapped they have become.

We all cry at certain eventualities that occur in our lifetime. As we gain a deeper and mature insight into the human mind, we find crying is an expression of self-pity. Our sentimental feelings make us feel sorry for ourselves. If a loved one has died we no longer have that person around to share our love and physical actions with. The person we are crying over has gone in physical form so we cannot be crying for them. It is our view of how we see the situation we are crying over.

When someone is sick or dying, crying may ease the tension we feel brought on by the stressful situation of watching loved ones wasting away in physical form. Tears do relieve tension, but they also leave us with a headache and feelings of melancholy.

If we allow our loved ones to see worry and crying this worsens their plight. Their healing mechanism depends on a positive energy flow.

If we truly love them then we would never inflict our negative worry to add to their critical state.

The most selfish act one human can inflict on another is to give them their worry. We all have concern and consideration for our loved ones. The only real lasting way to council and help is our *Spiritual* energy that has healing powers emitting from joy and love.

Having and holding an inner joy is our daily focus. If we allow ourselves to be sidetracked by the man-made ego, then crying and worry will become a habit we cannot break.

It is a constant learning process on how to remain a bright light and ascend to higher levels of divine bliss. This is the reason we exist. This lesson must remain our priority while we are on earth.

LOOKING FOR THE LIGHT

Forces of ego's caress, a course in aggressiveness,
attachments to pride and arrogance, my what a mess,
manipulating and vengeful, no mercy to harness,
a contempt of love, self-pity and suffering to bless.

Attacks from the religious fears and guilt appear to bind,
listening to judgments from a conditioned mind,
lifting the veil, jealousy and hatred is all we find,
martyrs to doom and gloom, too many strings to wind.

Lessons sought, faith and trust return,
surrender to the oneness, the mastery we learn,
no self-righteous selfishness, just love and concern,
sadness and hurt dissipate as the leaves of the book turn.

Hip, hip hooray, the conditioned brains on a holiday,
Release thoughts of negativity, the final act in play,
unity of self-power, delivered in Spirit's Way,
you know at last, the light of positivity is here to stay.

M.L.

Man and Tree

I was giving a lecture recently and was talking about man's connection to trees. A young man in the audience stood up and said he felt insulted that he should be compared to a tree. "I'm Human and a tree is a piece of wood" were his words.

Nearly every house in America, and many other countries throughout the world, are built from trees. If we never had wooden ships, then most Americans would not be Americans. All our paper comes from trees. Our tires come from rubber trees. People living on islands carve canoes from trees, use the leaves of trees both for roofing their homes and in the cooking of their foods. Many plates and containers were made of wood in primitive times, and wood is still used in carvings and bowls. Most of our fruit is grown on trees.

There is all the vegetation that supplies food for all animals and life forms. Most of all, we could not breath without trees and plants which help supply oxygen. Ninety-percent of man's molecules is the same as the tree.

The young man who asked the question now said, "I never looked at it like that, I just took it for granted." That is the problem with the society we live in today. We take things for granted and although it is simple to see our connection to trees, we do not think about it. That is the cause of all the destruction man is inflicting on earth.

Man has forgotten that we humans are connected to every tree, plant, ocean, every drop of water, every animal. If we continue to deplete and pollute Earth, we will shortly destroy ourselves.

The temperature of the Earth's crust is increasing yearly. Heavy industry pollutes our air and our water. We can still advance industry and hi-tech without polluting. A tree would never harm a human. Trees are our life. Love a tree as we would our children, for if we don't, our children will cease to exist.

As I write these words, we are coming to the end of 1998. This is New Years Eve and everyone is making their "New Year Resolutions."

ON REFLECTION

As we come to the end of an ordinary year,
so many things are still not clear,
my worries I tried to drown in beer,
never heeded the warning signs on the route I steer.

This year I thought I would go far,
here I am choking on a cigar,
some how or other good luck and I have not met,
I think I'll light another cigarette.

I can't get enough of chocolates, meat and cheese,
I don't exercise and my lungs have a funny wheeze,
my clothes no longer fit, my waist line is a tease,
I continue on the treadmill of life, for my friends I like to please.

The only Spirit I know is in a glass,
I buy all the new fancy toys, but the pleasure never lasts,
one day I might learn the right God to ask,
for now I'm lying in my hospital bed, with my oxygen mask.

M.L.

As we start a New Year, which will be the last in the Millennium, we must all take our minds on a *Spiritual Journey* of ecstasy for the remaining years of our lives. No artificial substitute can replace the contentment we can embrace within *Spirit*.

We can all make this world a better place to live in if we focus our minds on the joy of life. This joy encompasses all living entities on the Planet.

We must celebrate every day as we do New Year's Eve.

Every Eve is a celebration. When we celebrate every Eve with every Atom (Adam), we will live in the Garden of Eden.

PARTY TIME

Well tell me my dear what you think of this party,
I suppose it was okay but sometimes it did get a little naughty,
most of the guests did not realize the theme,
after all is said and done life is but a dream.

It started all right, but the joy seemed to drift from sight,
the chat turned to a debate of might then the fools began to argue and fight,
there were plenty of streamers and balloons,
but the musicians seemed to play all the wrong tunes.

The cake was too big we ate too large a slice,
it was okay while we munched, a little later it wasn't so nice,
too many choices it make our heads spin,
there was so much waste, most of the goodies ended in the garbage bin.

Now we've left the party and we're at the gate,
we no longer need fine clothes and we'll never be late,
we were taking our pick when our appointment came far too quick,
was there a theme or was it all a party trick.

M.L.

No Quick Fixes

Many different forms of counseling exist today to help us overcome unpleasant occurrences that invade our lives. The build-up of conditioning throughout our lives leads us down a path of mental self-destruction.

Nearly all illnesses manifest themselves from our ill-conceived ideas of who we think we are. Therefore, when we are in need of treatment, most practitioners will also use their ego as a reference point; so you have the situation of one ego treating another ego. This never lasts in the long run and further visits and different counselors are sought to try and solve ongoing problems.

Psychiatrists often give medication while trying to solve deep routed mental stress. When the condition has been allowed to progress to a high level of stress, then medications seems to be the only way to alleviate this condition so that some relief is found. This is only a temporary fix and unless the sufferer continues with medication the anxiety immediately returns. Who wants to be addicted to tablets the rest of their lives? They only treat the symptom not the cause.

Nearly all forms of counseling helps to overcome the immediate problem, but as we go through life our problems may differ and increase so solving one problem does not mean other occurrences will not become bothersome. When negative conditions persist for long periods of time, massive amounts of toxins are generating from the mind into a chemical imbalance in our bodies, leading to severe physical illness.

It can be compared to dieting. People try all types of fad diets and lose weight rapidly, only to put it all back again in a few months plus a few extra pounds. There are no quick fixes for physical well-being. A sensible balanced diet and regular exercise is the only way to maintain a healthy body.

It's the same way with our minds. The only way to a joyful contented fulfilling life is to acknowledge we are more than just flesh and blood. That all the materialistic wealth that is in our world has a very limited meaning. In fact, in the Cosmic picture it has no meaning at all.

Our Soul is our guiding light. By attaching our thought process to a higher level of existence. It will take away all the stress of modern living. Contentment of just being alive with no preconditions other than enjoying the present moment alleviates worry and anxiety. It is not something that can be tried for a short period of time then go back to our past conditioning. It is a daily exercise of clearing our mind of the clutter that continually bombards us.

LIFE IN A BOTTLE

A lifetime of being all bottled up,
Reading the leaves in a teacup,
How many times does the stomach churn,
Ending on a shelf, this is what we 'urn.'

Tense and taught, balancing on a tight rope,
Searching in the dark, seeing how we grope,
Follow the leader who's brainwashed by the media,
Having no chance to grow, life becomes seedier.

Always with a want, demand and expect,
Disappointment is the result, that's all we get,
Backing all the losers, societies rules, not a fare bet,
Swallowed by anxiety, buried in futile debt.

A glimmer of hope turns to a ray of sunshine,
A beaming light from our Soul's divine,
An endless flow we soak up and relax,
God and Spirit verses death and tax.
                                    M.L.

Every day we must accept our *Spirit* as our reality; this is our Eternal spark. *A spark is a thought and that is all we really are.* Do we want to be a bright spark or a dim one? This is the most important lesson any human being can learn. Do not be deterred. Transform to our Eternal being while we still have physical form.

It has always been with us; only now we are beginning to recognize it and follow the direction it leads us to. *That is divine blissfulness.* We find we live in a Magical Kingdom of sheer bliss. Nothing on earth can distract our flow of delight.

There are situations that we are made to face in our daily lives that could take our joy away if we let them. For instance, we have our in-laws coming to stay with us for a few weeks over a holiday period. We like the privacy of our own home, but our partner's parents are staying with us and invading our privacy. Not only that, they take what we give and can be critical. They do not seem to appreciate our kindness and do not reciprocate our giving.

Do we become resentful and off-hand leading to arguments or do we see a different side to this situation? Would we like to be the one who receives and not the giver?

We have been fortunate enough to be in a position of giving, and even though it does not seem to be appreciated, it is far better to be the giver rather than the receiver.

Have joy in giving and want nothing back in return.

Do not expect thanks, just do things out of the goodness of our hearts. *We will receive back in so many ways that may not seem obvious.* We immediately feel better by just thinking in this manner.

Just enjoying being a giver will alleviate a tremendous amount of stress.

Another example of how simple we can alleviate stress is the following situation. We all know someone who "gets on our nerves." It could be the boss or someone else at work. It could be a close friend who always dwells on the negative aspect of life; and when we are in a joyful state, they will say things to "wind us up" and make us angry about events we have no control over.

We cannot ignore their comments because they continue with their verbal attacks until our happiness disappears. They have succeeded in taking the joy of the day away by their misguided demanding approach to life.

IT'S A JUNGLE OUT THERE

Welcome to the circus, a Big Top to nurse,
performing to society's whims, no time to rehearse,
clowning with a conditioned mind, going from bad to worse,
tight rope round the throat making life perverse, jugglers with a fatal curse.

Welcome to the zoo, how do you moo,
push and shove, the animals walking all over you,
beggar thy neighbor, pigs wallowing in their own stew,
I'm all right jack, hyenas laughing in their own pew
with a stubborn view.

Welcome to the jungle, dear heart,
see how we savages are ripped apart by thought,
predators who pray, the innocent get caught,
venom from the mouth, the diseased minds bought.

Welcome to the giants lair,
Fee, Fie, Foe, Fum, watch out! take care!
The monster "negativity" will strip your joy quite bare,
use all your senses for bliss, time to become aware.

Angers are trampled, by the hooves of a fool,
kind words ignored by the actions of the mule,
snakes in the grass know how to be cruel,
destroy all the good is their uncaring rule.
                                              M.L.

When we are in tune with our Soul no amount of badgering from negative people or situations will take our joy away. We explain to the "winder upper" that they need to release their conditioned mind and learn to enjoy the moment, time is precious.

You will find that negative people will either change for the better and want more information on how to live life in joy, or they will avoid meeting us. They will leave us alone and find like-minded negative people to associate with.

We will be classed as cranks and will be regarded as not quite normal. They will tell other people that we are dangerous or spooky and try to discredit our way of thinking.

We know we are on the correct *Spiritual* path when negative people regard us as *"not normal."* Who wants to be normal by society's materialistic standards. *No truly successful person in "the art of living" needs to compare with anyone else.*

They have their power supplied by God and they are aware of it. It encompasses the whole of Earth and who can be alone when connected to so much energy with so much to teach us.

Indeed in our lifetime we can only learn a little of all this intelligence that is ours for the taking. *We gratefully and thankfully accept all God's gifts. This power is all we ever need to receive. Everything else fades into insignificance.*

BLUE CHIP BRAIN WAVES

Zim! zam! ali kazam! filters of a miracle
sparks of thought whiz, bang, wham,
dimension zip within a Cosmic Scan,
Celestial wave bands, in a flair conditioned fan.

Incredible forces not known to man,
fabulous mysteries, no publishers have ran,
gift of gold, in our treasured sphere,
an invisible force, our wholly atmosphere.

Silent codes, no S.O.S. from morse,
brain waves sent through matters on a course,
somewhere in space, a Universal Spirit Force,
radio and gamma, the tip of the unicorn horse.

Ancient and modern currents, no new trick,
exaltation of knowledge, a zap of electric,
pools of energy, platters of heavenly delight,
steaming cauldron of joy, cells with bites of might.

Distant views, waiting for a visions gaze,
flashes to set ones mind ablaze,
dancing wisps with laser speed faze,
"blue chip brain waves", mountains of glory days.

M.L.

Oh what joy and bliss can be found once our conditioned minds become reprogrammed. We are now tuned into the *"Power of Joy"* channel. Our fairy tales come true. *Once Upon Our Time* and lasts for **ALL TIME**.

When we hear a good opera tenor hit those high notes a tingle goes through our body. When we taste a terrific food for the first time, our taste buds explode and a magnificent sensation travels through our body. When we make love and feel a phenomenal orgasm, the sensation travels throughout our body and seems to lift us to a place beyond this Earth. When we meditate and find silence, our sensations go to higher levels of blissfulness.

When we tune into our Soul and connect to the Cosmic flow which we call God, these sensations take us to ever increasing high levels of exultation -- of supreme bliss. No amount of devastation or pain in our human existence can interfere with this divine bliss. It is in another dimension and we can live in this dimension at the same time as playing our role on earth.

Read these words over and over until living them becomes natural. Only then can we be regarded as truly normal and this is in God's eyes.

The Wind

There is a force that is invisible to the eye yet no one can deny it exists. We feel the wind on our cheek as we walk in the fresh air, but do we really think of the significance of the wind.

The wind carves out the shape of the Earth. Through eons of years, mountains have turned to plains by the wind's erosion. Our Planet constantly erodes and corrodes by wind, vapors and heat. Vapors and heat can be seen as water and fire but the wind remains invisible.

Hurricanes and tornadoes are examples of the forces the wind can extract. The seas can be whipped into a frenzy and tidal waves can cover large land masses with the wind's force. As time goes by land will become ocean and oceans will become land. Ever changing, nothing stands still. Humans come, humans go. Just as the wind is an invisible force we may define our Souls as the wind.

The Soul comes into the body for a short period then leaves with information collected from the human matter. The Soul's power is enormous, far stronger than any hurricane, and can travel through space in dimensions not known to mankind.

The force and speed is faster than light, an everlasting journey in an infinite place, non-local, forever and ever. Mind boggling thoughts.

The wind portrays how invisible forces have such great power. Power no human can control. Humans are no match for the force of nature and the forces we see on this planet are merely a puff of smoke in comparison to the power of *Spirit*.

The next time we feel the wind blow on our cheek think of the power we hold inside our bodies. We possess the miracle of life and have use of all this great power. However, most humans ignore the simplicity of it all. The more simple our thought, the greater our power.

FACED WITH JOY !

A life times anguish, each wrinkle portrays,
every line on the face, worry has fazed,
anger between the ears, eyes that blaze,
a mind lost, in a negative foggy haze.

A surgeon's scalpel, a plastic change of look,
memories are still written in your book,
there is no escape from the route you took,
a pretty face, but still burnt offerings you cook.

Going around, with your chin on the ground,
mouth turned down, only troubles found,
king of the fools, now you have been crowned,
crying out loud, alas an empty sound.

A face with joy, never needs to alter,
always a positive thought, a ray of light without falter,
savoring every crease, each line is bliss so dear,
the mind is youthful, strong, Soulful and clear.

M.L.

We manufacture a host of negative nonsense that fill the brain with meaningless rubbish, which just erodes and corrodes into the nothingness it came from. The Soul has no use for it. The Soul only encompasses joy, love and all the sensations and exultation that stem from them.

The sensations we feel through our senses are transmitters to the brain and then transmitted by our Souls into eternity. Language does not exist in eternity. Only sensations of positive or negativity exist in the *True World*. This dimension of existence is one of billions of dimensions that are all connected. *We are a strand in these dimensions.*

This level of existence can be experienced here on Earth once we clear away the clutter of the mind and start to achieve the sensations of *divine bliss*. The words we read in this book will allow us to start our journey.

If we allow our mind to use our Soul as the reference point of wisdom, then we feel the sheer pleasure of *divine blissfulness*.

Play the Game – Round One

How do we know when we are happy? We all love things in life like shopping, sports, going to the movies. Let us analyze a few and see if these make us happy. Sports - I like to play golf so we will talk about that. We go on the golf course to enjoy ourselves. I play golf with some very successful people -- doctors, lawyers and businessmen.

They go out to enjoy themselves on the golf course but as soon as they hit a bad shot they are down on themselves. Calling themselves names like dummy, idiot, etc. If anyone else spoke to them like this there would be an argument; but they take this abuse from themselves all in the name of enjoying a sport.

The same goes for any other sport we play. We are rarely, if ever, going to play to our full potential. We can always play better, so being dissatisfied with our performance should really not take the enjoyment away; but it does. Remember getting all excited about going to a casino or racetrack? Buying stocks on the stock market has turned into a bigger gamble than the casino or racetrack.

We are happy when we are on a winning streak, but when do we stop? How far do we push it? Who is clever enough to know when to hold and when to fold? Only a real wizard can work that out. The outcome is rarely what we envision.

Many people like to go shopping. We get all excited buying a new product, jewelry, clothing, cars, or electrical goods. What happens to the clothing once we have worn it once or twice? We can't wait to get the clutter out of our closets.

There is always a new model automobile that we must have so the old one gets discarded after a few years. The majority of us look forward to our yearly holiday. We are working hard all year for one or two weeks for fun in the sun. When the time comes we have delayed flights, stolen baggage, sunstroke and many other "enjoyable" things to contend with.

We call home and tell the folks what a great time we are having. It seldom lives up to our expectations. We lie to ourselves by pretence of enjoyment when all the time we are suffering.

RISKY LIES

A venture in a game of chance,
A risk which may or may not enhance,
Travel through life in a meaningless amble,
A paradox of proof, taking a gamble.

Allowing sordid revelations to persist,
Happiness on the top of our most wanted list,
A quest for truth, variations on veracity,
Minds filled with lies, exploding beyond their capacity.

Omissions of the real, shuffle a phony deal,
A misguided vision, with egos strong as steel,
Flaky bits of crust, soon begin to rust,
A forsaken Soul, no room for faith and trust.

Dazzling "Bolts of Blue," reflecting heavenly bliss,
White magic sparks fly, love embraces it's divineness,
Blinded by the light, deceptions of the mind take flight,
Invisible oneness, becomes our real truth and might.

M.L.

So where do we find our true happiness? We need to be able to sit on our own porch in quiet contentment and just be happy with everything we see around us. We are never going to find true happiness with all the man-made stuff.

With no attachments to the materialistic world and no great wants, we begin to achieve feelings of happiness and true contentment. Then when we do go out to play our sport we can still enjoy the challenges; with the difference being we enjoy the bad games too. *They make the good ones seem so much better.*

The shopping expeditions can be enjoyed, but we look on it as a bonus, the "icing on the cake" and that's all. It still doesn't beat the contentment of sitting on the porch looking at the moon and stars, plants and flowers and helping our fellow man.

As for the stock market, etc., who cares. It doesn't really matter what's going on with things we have no control over. The best advice I was ever given was to enjoy the bad deals as much as the good. It took a little time to understand what this meant. *There is no such thing as a bad deal in life. Everything in life is a learning experience.*

Even the severest pain has to be embraced, not in the context of the pain but in the fact that most of our life is lived without pain. The pain is sent as a wake up call to make us appreciate that just being alive in physical form is enough to gain divine bliss. The sooner we learn these lessons the sooner we know what true happiness is. Let's get back to the golf.

PLAYING A ROUND

The sun is rising, I yawn and stretch,
no work today, no need to carry and fetch,
eight o'clock tee time, now for an enjoyable golf round,
can't wait to get started, my rhythm I have found.

On the first tee, swing through the ball,
skied in the air, it went nowhere at all,
finished the hole, with a lousy eight,
all of a sudden, I don't feel so great.

Next hole will be better, on the green in two,
four putts makes me a silly moo,
what a daft game to pursue,
in a few more holes, I may change my view.

At the end of nine, I'm tired and weary,
what a dummy, I tell myself so surly,
my glasses were steamed up, I couldn't see clearly,
fifty-two strokes out, I got up too early.

Things go from bad to worse, now I'm beginning to curse,
the wind blows on my cheek, my Soul takes a peek,
the last hole a par three, a good swing, where did that come from,
OH MY GOD!!! a hole in ONE.

At last the nineteenth hole, now I have a big grin,
life's for fun, so I'll take it on the chin,
I possess an inner glow, there's no need of a Gin,
all the rounds of life, Spirit helps me win.

M.L.

Play the Game -- Round Two

One of my hobbies for the past thirty years is golf. I have been a middle handicap golfer for many years and my present handicap is sixteen. This morning I tried an experiment. I decided that Michael Levy would be left out of the game; he was just there as a spectator.

On the first nine holes Michael kept interfering in the game. When he poked his nose in, short putts were missed and bad shots were hit. Very good shots were hit when he did not interfere. On the next nine holes a transformation occurred.

Michael kept out of the game completely. The score for that nine was thirty-eight, two over par. I never shot such a low score before. I also realized it was not Michael that shot the low score. It was the Universal Energy force that used the body. The conditioned mind was told to keep out and it did.

My partner this day is a brilliant man. I respect his opinion on most subjects. He is extremely successful when it comes to financial matters and takes a very keen interest in all aspects of nature. I find this man to be extremely *Spiritual*. He told me he is an atheist and all things happen by chance.

He does not recognize his *Spirit*. He has an ego that is not showy. He does not care about other people's opinion. If he does not agree, he will not argue. He is very self-contained; he wants to achieve excellence in all he does and his ego is only directed at himself. He is a low handicap golfer, almost at professional standard but for a mental glitch. His short chips cannot be controlled. His mind - as brilliant as it is - will not allow him to make the simplest shot. The hard long shots are allow him to make the simplest shot. The hard long shots are no problem, but for years the simple short shot has plagued him.

Away from the golf course we all carry a handicap. Most of us are of average intelligence. Only a few people have a very high I.Q., and are often professors, scientists, brain surgeons, etc. All these people still carry a handicap. They cannot be in joy twenty four hours a day. Who can?

We all can. By releasing the conditioning within our minds we can lower our handicap in life. Each layer of conditioning we strip away will give us a better shot at enjoying our lives.

When we become professional at life we have no handicap. This does not mean we are going to be happy twenty-four hours a day. It means we have the ability to do so but we have to practice every day. If we lose our concentration on any day, a worry or anxiety will add a shot to our handicap.

The secret to a good life is to allow *Spirit* to mark our card and play all the shots for us. When our ego comes into play, we have a disastrous round. We have to go back to the practice range to learn our swing over again. In other words, we need meditation to tune into our power source to get back to no handicap.

Once we lose the feel for *Spirit*, it may take quite a while for our joy to return. Devastation can be hard to recover from; but as with the good golfer, if you know you have a good swing, it is only a matter of time before we play good golf again. We must learn that the simple things in life are the best, they do not require money just contentment, peace and tranquility. The simple shot is often the hardest if we cannot clear the mind of conditioned clutter.

With *Spirit* as our coach and player, how can we possibly go wrong? It takes the three P's - *practice, patience* and *perseverance* to achieve a life filled with joy and happiness. The brain surgeon and the warehouse janitor can both be equal in their joy of the day. We can all become professional players in the *"Life of Joy"* contest.

When we finally play our last round, we will take all those joyful days with us to our *Eternal Club*. The nineteenth hole will fill our glass with our own divine *Spirit*.

The Magic Elixir

We listen to the news on the television and a startling new drink has been discovered that has special qualities and it assures us of good health. It will alleviate all worry and anxiety. It tastes good. It is free; it will not cost us a dime. We can have as many drinks in a day as we please and it has no detrimental side effects. It will put us on a higher level of joy than alcohol or drugs, and when taken regularly, we will never need another headache tablet.

The drink is *Spirit* and we will call it by a different name a little later. I know a lot of people who would refuse to drink it. They would say it is impossible for a drink to perform miracles. They say God does not exist. When we die that is the end of everything for us. No other form of existence can be.

Now what would they have to lose by drinking this magic potion? It costs nothing, it has no side effect other than joy and happiness, love and contentment. It is habit forming and once we get hooked on it we will never want to give it up. Luckily we have a great supply. We are going to call this magic potion *water*. It falls from the sky and seventy-percent of our body is water.

It has already performed miracles, for without water, no life would exist in physical form. Now we are going to allow water to perform another miracle and let us see existence in a *Spiritual* form; the form that is everlasting. *It has no beginning and no end.* We are just a physical interlude in an ever-playing melody. A constant flow with a brief physical presence to receive and transmit information of physical life before returning to *The Eternal Melody*.

TIME IS A BARGAIN

Roll up, roll up for the bargain of the year,
forty to sixty-percent off if you get buried here,
what a deal, you can't beat that.
If you can, I'll eat my hat.

Got a lot of money then you'll get a good plot,
get a big casket and pile in everything you've got,
you've been a miser and worried a lot,
you deserve the best but the best you forgot.

A mis-spent life is quite fine,
at your funeral there was a big line,
people wept and some did pine,
then off they trot to drink your finest wine.

If you live your life without joy,
you've fallen for the devil's ploy,
be a simple soul let Spirit be your toy,
then you can live like a happy little girl and boy.

The best things in life are really quite free,
a jolly outlook gives peace and harmony,
humans really are only a laugh and a joke,
sing like a frog for far too soon we will have to croak.

M.L.

When we drink a glass of water it reminds us who we are. Just as water flows in a river or stream. Just as water ebbs and flows in the seas and oceans. We flow on an eternal current of energy in an infinite space called the Cosmos. Each glass of water is a reminder that we have a limited time in our physical form.

Every second is a precious jewel. Every drop of water is a God given gift. We must not spill a drop. We must not waste a second. No more time for worry or anxiety. The water is the magic elixir reminding us of our Soul. Medical science tells us we need to drink eight to twelve eight-ounce glasses of fluid a day.

Now every time we have a drink of water we are going to remember our *Spirit*, especially if things are not going the way we like and pressure is mounting. Deadlines need to be met. We're late for an appointment. We have an important interview. We have to make a speech.

As we drink a glass of water we allow our minds to take us into the flow of life in the physical and life in the *Spiritual* together. *The Soul will allow the physical unfettered joy; to enjoy the day no matter what. Remember, no "Matter" Lasts.*

CROPS OF THOUGHT

A crop of thought, in a field of dreams,
succulent tastes of a summers day radiate from silver streams,
bathed in beauty, floating in an inner glow,
an ocean of conscious bliss, within my Eternal Flow.

Impulse movements of wishes and desire,
divinity in vapors heat, rising higher to inspire,
notes of harmonious cords, sailing on a gentle breeze,
mind and matter entwined, swaying in willowy trees.

Fantasy in sparkling crystal quartz, diamond facets shine,
timeless sparks in the blessed eternal flame mine,
infra red, ultra violet, all colors infusing a rainbow,
sensitive memories, inscribed in a Soul's photo.

Reflections flash, in the eye of space,
exulted joy emerging from an angels face,
tissues and sinew filled with peaceful tranquility,
Spirit's presence living in magnificent simplicity.
M.L.

Conclusion

In a fast moving world full of man-made ideologies, it is important we can rest in our own temple -- an inner sanctum of quiet contentment; a place that has no intrusion of nonsense from the physical world in which we live. Peace and harmony abide in a warm paradise.

In silent meditation we realize this is who we really are. Love and joy are our sensations of pure bliss.

All the beauty we see on Earth in nature is a reflection of the beauty that is in all humans. Our inner feelings are joy and bliss encompassing all the beauty in our world and the sky and stars. We are nature's miracle and we must love every molecule and atom. We must search the deep recesses of our mind and soak up the pleasure and treasure of life. Joy is in every tree, flower, blade of grass and every drop of our blood.

May you always live in joy.

Here are twenty proverbs to help us find joy.

BOOK OF PROVERBS

Neither a borrower or lender be,
release the shackles to be free,
stuck in debt, is not for you or me,
be a free note, in a cord of harmony.

Look before you leap, don't get in too deep,
mountains of worry are too steep,
be "aware" or else you'll have to weep.

A stitch in time saves nine,
being a loose thread can make you whine,
procrastination has no reason or rhyme,
sew up the seams and you'll do just fine.

Fools rush in where angels fear to tread,
when ego rules the mind, it leads to lives of dread,
gives you a headache, in a dull and sluggish head,
when "Spirit" shines the light, it shows the road ahead.

Act in haste, repent at leisure,
what looks golden, isn't always a treasure,
size it up, get its measure,
then you'll make life, just a pure pleasure.

Many a slip between lip and cup,
life sometimes needs a nip and a tuck,
positive thinking gets you out of the muck,
in this world, you make your own luck.

Don't run before you can walk,
never get involved with "Big Time" talk,
be alert! rise up with the lark,
be well informed, then you'll be up to the mark.

From little acorns large oak trees grow,
it all depends on the seed that you sow,
make sure you know the right field to mow,
then you will be in the Spiritual flow.

It never rains, it always pours,
that does not mean you have to stay indoors,
when things go wrong without any understandable cause,
smile! Be happy to be alive, follow Cosmic Laws.

The more you have, the more you need,
don't become a collector of greed,
you only possess one mouth to feed,
spread your wealth around, do a good deed.

Birds of a feather stick together,
negative minds are not very clever,
a bigot's skin is as thick as leather,
a cloudy brain dwells in bad weather.

Cream will always rise to the top,
positive thinking makes us top of the crop,
a joyful mind makes worry pop!
"Spirit" uses negativity as a mop.

Too many cooks spoil the broth,
being a "busy body" makes the devil scoff,
mixing with toxic people can lead to a cough,
too much coughing, can lead to a coffin.

Let he who is without sin, cast the first stone,
demeaning others, makes the attacker prone,
if you don't forgive, your own sins will come home,
then you'll be attacked, and oh! how you'll groan.

Never swim against the tide,
fighting with nature should not be tried,
go with the flow, let your Soul be your guide,
don't tell lies, then you'll have nothing to hide.

Pride comes before a fall,
don't allow ego to make the call,
never try to break through a brick wall,
live a simple life, then you'll always walk tall.

Every cloud has a silver lining,
Smile! and the sun will keep shining,
keep happy, there's no time for whining,
one step at a time, the ladder of joy, we keep climbing.

A friend in need is a friend indeed,
expect too much, you will never succeed,
they'll turn you down, no matter how much you plead,
be self-reliant, make a flower grow from a weed.

All that glitters is not gold,
don't be fooled into debt, real treasures cannot be sold,
keep away from the 'Loan A-ranges,'
or the sharks will Hi! Ho! Your Silver away, and leave you in danger.

Happy all the time, well over the past,
never allow bad memories to last,
We know life passes far too fast,
be a star performer, in a happy cast.

The Joy of Life

In my life I've played many roles,
When I came to the crossroads I paid all the tolls,
I look to the future but no one can tell me what it holds,
Looking back my past has too many creases and folds.

I know I have the moment, it is precious and dear,
The song birds notes are music to my ear,
Visions of beauty within a rose appear,
The trees send me messages that are quite sincere.

I walk down the path along life's root,
I realize the simple way was my most enjoyable pursuit,
As the ocean flows my dreams came and went,
Happiness in all things is the gift I've been sent.

On the heels of endeavor, I derive my pleasure,
My work is called Joy, it does not change with the weather,
To feel the hail, rain or shine, makes everything sublime,
For embedded in me, is God's Love Divine.

ORDER FORM

Please send me _____ copies of "Enjoy Yourself: It's Later Than You Think."
By Michael Levy at a price of $9.95 each.
            Total $_____

Shipping and Handling
  First book - USA $3.50
       - Overseas $5.00
  Add $1 for each additional book
    Total shipping & handling $_____

Florida residents add 6% sales tax $_____

        TOTAL $_____

Customer Name _____
Customer Address _____
     _____
     _____

Telephone ( ) _____
e-mail   _____

All orders must be accompanied by payment.
Only checks in U.S. dollars drawn on a U.S. bank will accepted.

Orders should be sent to:
Point of Life, Inc.
Order Department
P.O. Box 7017
West Palm Beach, FL 33405
Tel: (561)655-1442 Fax: (561)655-5437
Prices are subject to change.

OR order from our web site: www.pointoflife.com